Arielle Jodine – Singer-Songwriter, Former
Imagine a world where young creatives are so confid
nothing can stop them! If you read this book and car
for what you make and create, I think the world w

Shannon Schultz – Author, Watercolour Artist, Painter
On the Edge of Greatness by Heidi Korte is not so much a 'cuddle under the covers with a cup of tea' kind of book but rather a valuable tool that should be kept close at hand by any and all creatives. It's the sort of book that invites scribbles and highlighters to mark the pages. It is full of testimonies by musicians, painters, and writers, reminding you that you are not alone in your struggle, and even better, some solutions are offered! The narrative will resonate with creatives from across a multitude of disciplines as Heidi shares with integrity, compassion, and vulnerability. This is a great companion guide when you find yourself standing on the edge of greatness!

JoAnn McFatter – Singer, Songwriter, Recording Artist
I have come to know, trust, and respect Heidi Korte, and I highly recommend her book to artisans just beginning as well as seasoned ones. Most likely, the latter have learned a lot of this the hard way—ha!—but the reminder does us all well. She has gotten to the point of issues we have all dealt with and that we continue to have pop into our heads at a moment's notice. Surprise! Many of these challenges can paralyze us or . . . if we look them straight in the eye . . . can thrust us forward in our journey. If you find yourself 'stuck,' you may very well find the key here if you dare to be honest with your creative self. Many will benefit from reading this book, and there is a good chance you will be among them.

Julie Meyer – Songwriter, Recording Artist,
Author of *30 Days of Praying the Psalms, and Singing the Scriptures*
I love this book. *On the Edge of Greatness* is an equipping tool for all creatives. Heidi Korte brings each reader on her journey through the depths of defeat to the heights of personal breakthrough, dedication, and right motivation, along with the pure joy of embracing every challenge, then simply turning it into triumph. Thank you, Heidi, for this book. I highly recommend this to anyone wanting to grow in their craft. If you are a beginner, read this book. If you are somewhere in the middle of your creative journey, read this book. If you are highly skilled, stay humble, and read this book. One will only get better by embracing each chapter and being encouraged by real and raw stories from many of Heidi's students as well as her own journey in becoming a highly skilled creative.

ON THE EDGE OF GREATNESS

REMOVING MENTAL BLOCKS THAT KILL CREATIVITY

HEIDI KORTE

One Printers Way
Altona, MB R0G 0B0
Canada

www.friesenpress.com

Copyright © 2023 by Heidi Korte
First Edition — 2023

Illustrations drawn by Iris Bjornson and Haven Peckover
Illustrations digitally remastered by Haven Peckover

All rights reserved.

No part of this publication may be reproduced in any form, or by any means, electronic or mechanical, including photocopying, recording, or any information browsing, storage, or retrieval system, without permission in writing from FriesenPress.

ISBN
978-1-03-916454-3 (Hardcover)
978-1-03-916453-6 (Paperback)
978-1-03-916455-0 (eBook)

1. Young Adult Nonfiction, Inspirational & Personal Growth

Distributed to the trade by The Ingram Book Company

*To my students who have shared their stories in this book.
I have never been prouder of all of you than at this moment.*

TABLE OF CONTENTS

ix	Introduction
xiii	Preface
1	Chapter 1: An Honest Look Through the Cobwebs of My Past
7	Chapter 2: Changing False Belief Systems
17	Chapter 3: Having the Right Motivation
27	Chapter 4: Identity and Self-Worth
33	Chapter 5: Fear
45	Chapter 6: Comparison
55	Chapter 7: Rejection
63	Chapter 8: Feedback and Who Should Give It to You?
71	Chapter 9: Perfectionism
81	Chapter 10: Displaying Process and Getting Over Embarrassment
89	Chapter 11: Self-Discipline
101	Chapter 12: Distractions and Time Management
109	Chapter 13: Avoidance
115	Chapter 14: Rushing to get the Job Done
123	Chapter 15: Schedule Overload
129	Chapter 16: The Land of the Halfway Finished Projects
135	Chapter 17: The Mopey Place
143	Chapter 18: You Become What You Listen To
147	Chapter 19: Arrogance and Self-Sufficiency
153	Chapter 20: The Artistic Orphan Mindset
159	Chapter 21: Creativity

167	Chapter 22: Problems Creating
177	Chapter 23: Keep Dreaming, Live in Reality
185	Chapter 24: It's Too Late for Me, Imposter Syndrome, and a Potpourri of Self-Doubt
193	Chapter 25: Sisu
197	Chapter 26: The Great Sacrifices
211	Chapter 27: Social Media Avoidance
217	Chapter 28: Advice from Professionals in the Field
227	Chapter 29: Closing Thoughts and a Good Mouse Story
231	Endnotes
233	Thank You

INTRODUCTION

Welcome, creatives! I am so happy you have found my book. *On the Edge of Greatness* is a gift from myself and my music studio, and I hope it brings you ascension into new levels of freedom and joy in your creative journey. These pages are filled with my practical instruction, along with my students' authenticity and vulnerability as they share pieces of their hearts with you. You'll also be hearing from professional creatives in different artistic fields about what hinders their creativity and how they overcome those things. Each of them has something valuable to give away so that you will realize you are not alone on your journey as a creative navigating the artistic world.

The student stories come from young musicians, but as creative people, we often wrestle with the same internal struggles, so I am confident that you dancers, painters, actors, poets, writers, and visual artists can translate the students' experiences and wisdom into your own fields of expertise. I would even go so far as to say that anyone involved in something that requires continued dedication, skill development, and self-confidence would benefit from reading this book.

This book does not delve into coping with mental illnesses like bipolar disorder or schizophrenia—if you are walking through one of these things, I want you to know you absolutely have your own place at the table of creativity, and a licensed psychologist, psychological nutritionist, and doctor are the people to go to for help managing these conditions—but this book deals with the mental obstacles that creatives face on a daily basis. After ten years of teaching music, I have come to believe that at least eighty percent of success in the arts has to do with success in the mind.

Most new students come into my music studio with large internal roadblocks that are directly connected to their craft. I don't have to probe for them either. The obstacles come up all by themselves in a lesson when they break down after making a mistake, cry when they sing wrong notes, or just can't seem to get into a regular practicing routine. That is the moment we begin the work. Those snares in their mind prevent them from moving forward in skill, shy them away from sharing their art, and keep them circling the base of the mountain of creativity rather than climbing to the top of it. As I have had the privilege of walking alongside students like these, helping them shed the scaly skins of negativity, comparison, or fear, I almost always see their artistic productivity and creativity ramp up as a result. I would even go so far as to say that their happiness level increases in their day-to-day lives.

Our art is a part of us, and if our creativity is suffering or constrained, we feel that deeply. Emotional obstacles in our creativity are often directly linked with other parts of our lives, and when we achieve freedom from them in the creative sense, often we receive a good measure of personal freedom as well. For example: fear of what other people think of our creations. When we overcome that artistically, it can't help but leak out into other aspects of our lives. Then fear of what other people think might have less of a hold over our whole situation. Wow, how amazing is that?!

The main obstacles I have come across in teaching and in my own life are centred around bigger themes: negativity and perfectionism, fear and anxiety, pride and self-sufficiency, lack of skill, and lack of self-discipline or follow-through. We will be talking about others as well, but I will not be addressing lack of skill in this book because that is something that you can work on by being in lessons, working with an instructor, or watching tutorials on YouTube. Your teachers and mentors will be the brilliant ones to guide you into areas of excellence in your desired field.

Something you will see referenced from my students and I throughout this book is 'Pass the Performance,' and I want to give you a quick explanation.

When the global pandemic began in 2020, most of the artistic world took a big hit as live performances and events were shut down. I decided that my students were going to sing and perform more than they ever had before, but online. As well as filming a full studio music video for YouTube (*Opening Up—A Waitress Parody*), we started performing every day on our studio Instagram. I christened it 'Pass the Performance' or 'PTP' for short. My music studio posted a performance every single day from April 15, 2020, to August 31, 2021. That's five hundred days in a row (and so very much texting and reminding from me)! I did this for a number of reasons. Reason one, coronavirus afforded me the unique opportunity to chip away at fear and insecurity in the majority of my students. Normally, my music studio would do a live show twice a year, but this group of students learned and performed a song a month for a year and a half straight. Performing and introducing themselves online was so scary for them at first. It was going to be there 'forever' for 'all their friends to see.' In years past, if they botched a live performance, they could forget it ever happened once they deleted their parents' video recordings. Online was a different situation entirely. But when you do something that is terrifying over and over again, usually it becomes less terrifying. For almost all of them, this created a positive circle of peer pressure. Normally, peer pressure is described as a negative thing, but in this instance, no one wanted to be the one performer that broke the cycle for the group, so PTP forced them to learn new music, practice hard, and have an entire song ready each month on their day. Either that or they learned a song last minute, performed it sloppily in their pyjamas, were embarrassed, and learned another valuable lesson: to be more prepared for the next month (which is also a great learn for the real music world)! Failure, as I will go into detail about later, is a really good friend and teacher of mine.

I also insisted that students send me their bloopers to post on our Instagram story on the day of their performance. I did this intentionally for a variety of reasons. First, they are hilarious, and I love them so much. Bloopers brought smiles to so many faces during a time when we all needed a laugh and some joy. Second, bloopers show process. If you want to grow beyond student shows in your desired field, you will need to learn to be comfortable showing process instead of hiding away until you think you are 'good enough.' With PTP, I wanted to create a safe place where even my beginner musicians who couldn't quite keep a tune yet were allowed to participate and feel celebrated for where they were at.

In my experience teaching, I have found that the students who hide away until they are 'good enough' continue to hide even when they are in fact 'good enough.' Their fear doesn't dissipate with the increase in skill, it is actually a separate thing that needs to be addressed for what it is: often a fear of displaying imperfection and a fear of rejection for it. The bloopers were a part of my students' learning process, and they also conveyed to the rest of the group that they weren't the only ones 'making mistakes over and over again.' Quite a few of my students believed they were the only ones not getting things perfectly right away. Our bloopers morphed mistakes into something to be laughed at instead of panicked or cried about. Who my PTP students have become a year and a half later is pretty remarkable. If you are ever in need of some good chuckles, we have over seven hundred bloopers up on our Instagram highlights @heidikortesmusicstudio, guaranteed to put a smile on your face when you are in need of one.

PREFACE

In my experience growing up, mental health was something that was not talked about. Even through my university music studies in the early 2000s, it was not discussed or mentioned even once. Mental health is essential for survival as a creative, and let's face it, we don't just want to survive as creatives, we want to thrive! We create and express ourselves the easiest when we are at peace with ourselves. Have you ever tried to create something in a slumpy, dismal mindset? I have found that what comes out of me in those moments isn't usable. The same thing often happens if I am anxious and try to write lyrics. There is a stall when I panic, and swirling thoughts get in the way of my creative flow. In a calmer moment, when I am grounded, I can put words and music to that anxiety or dark feeling in a way that expresses it. In a peaceful or joyful moment, ideas and imagination seem to flourish or flow effortlessly like a river. Part of our mission as creatives is to learn to access that river whenever we want to and move past the things in our mind that hinder us from exploring it.

Furthermore, because what we do as artists usually manifests as a product—a thing that is liked or disliked by others, is critiqued, succeeds or fails, and can be rejected—our sense of self-worth needs to be stable and not coupled with our performance or product. In order to survive having precious, deep parts of us graded by other people all the time, it is essential we creatives become experts at mental and emotional fortitude. Whether someone likes your work or not, or how many views you get on YouTube, my hope is that this book will empower you to step out, triumph, and show off your work, your abilities, your process, and yes, even your failures, fearlessly.

This book will delve into the depths a lot of the time, so I really don't recommend reading it all in one sitting. I would suggest reading a chapter, doing some reflection after, and then taking some time to let it absorb. Internal work cannot be rushed. Each chapter will be dealing with an obstacle, its root, some practical things you can do to overcome and manage it, as well as student stories and advice from other creatives. I highly recommend reading the chapter on lie-based thinking first because I will refer back to it in most other chapters.

It is my greatest hope that all of you reading this book, who are standing on the edge of greatness, can take the leap!

CHAPTER 1
AN HONEST LOOK THROUGH THE COBWEBS OF MY PAST

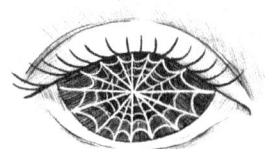 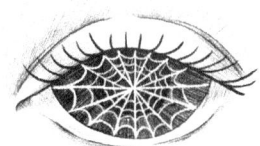

I want to start off by sharing my journey with you, highlighting where my mind crippled my ability to succeed. I believe in being open and transparent about my mistakes (as embarrassing as that is sometimes) so that my students don't have to go through the pain of making the same ones themselves, and so that my ceiling can be their floor. I think that should be the attitude of all teachers.

I spent the first nineteen years of my life in a small town in northeastern Ontario, Canada, about seven hours north of Toronto. There was a yearly music festival and quite a few people who were passionate about music, but local concerts were rare and there were no open mic nights and only a few musical instructors. We didn't have vocal jazz or musical theatre in high school either, so most singing was done through private lessons.

My mother put me in music lessons when I was very young, and I grew up being a pretty big fish in a small pond. This was a very comfortable place to be, and my personal value was rooted in the placement and marks I got from the annual music festival. My mother entered me in almost every class that I was eligible to participate in, and I walked away each year with money and a lot of red ribbons. I never placed lower than second and, full disclosure, the few times I placed second, I was devastated. It felt like the grade wasn't just a rank of how well I had performed that day, but a label that defined me as a person: not good enough. I needed to be the best, all the time, in order to have value. I saw any other singer with talent in my town as a threat to my own identity and often sat there in competitions praying that the other singers would fail miserably on stage so that there would be room for me to succeed. There it is, ugly, but honest. Keep reading.

Thank God for Gail Menard and Theresa McDermott, who ran the music programs in our town's junior and high schools. I played the tuba for five years and found a sense of belonging in the high school band community. "The tuba?" you ask. Yes, the tuba. In grade nine, I desperately wanted to go to California with the senior band, and I was conniving enough to find out they needed a tuba player the summer before high school. California was amazing. Moving on . . .

In high school, I was also fortunate enough to begin studying with Martha Collins, an amazing operatic vocal instructor from New York City. This was the nineties, so there was no Skype or FaceTime, and cellphones had not really come into vogue yet. I did vocal lessons over a landline telephone in my kitchen. I would sing something, and then go pick up the phone to hear what she thought of it. I trained my voice weekly over the phone while my parents went on walks since I was too embarrassed to have any voice cracks with them within earshot. As I write this, I am teaching on Zoom because of the pandemic, and when students complain about working virtually, I tell them it was nothing like the difficulties of studying over the telephone. I did landline lessons for five years before going to university to study voice. And I walked uphill in the winter both ways to do it too.

In moving to the big city for university, suddenly being the little fish in an enormous ocean of singers, who were all equally talented or better than me, was something I was not prepared for emotionally. I felt like I had lost my footing. I wanted all the other singers to think I was good and that I deserved to be there. When your self-worth is in your talent and all you want to do is impress people, the last thing you want to do is crack or wobble on a note in front of them. I was so scared of letting people see imperfection or failure in me that I hid away and sang as little as possible. Other students sang in recitals, made really embarrassing public mistakes, and grew from them. I withdrew. I rarely practiced or did my vocal exercises because the only place I had to rehearse were these gawd-awful practice rooms at school, which were not soundproof and were in earshot of everyone in all the classrooms on that side of the building. Even thinking about them today causes my stomach to tighten up. I remember sitting in those small, horrible spaces for hours, shouting internally at myself, "Come on, Heidi! Make a sound! SING SOMETHING!" then sitting there in silence until my hour was up.

My voice has an extremely weird high note flip into its whistle register (the Mariah Carey high notes). Instead of smoothly transitioning up like many of my students' voices can, my voice would go up/honk/crack to a random whistle note above that. It sounded like a goose honk. Super. Embarrassing. It is still a dicey thing for me to sing any of those transition notes without obsessively warming up first, and the odds are, it might still happen! In university, I was terrified to do my vocal exercises because I didn't want my peers to hear my goose honk. Honestly, if I was in a history class back then and heard someone else's voice cracking badly in the practice rooms, I would have smirked and felt superior.

At the end of a silent hour in those practice rooms, I would leave the music campus feeling totally defeated, hating myself for not being brave enough to warm up with an audience listening. Making embarrassing noises with your voice is scary enough at home by yourself, but as someone who had never worked on my confidence before, I was not prepared to humiliate myself in front of the entire music faculty. This led to a vicious cycle of not practicing, not being prepared, and avoiding singing—which was completely ridiculous since I was literally in university for singing! Looking back, it is a bit funny, but it is also painful to remember how deeply insecure I felt. At the end of my four-year bachelor's degree, I had accomplished very little. I had passed all my classes with honours, but I had no career in front of me, no job opportunities, and had wasted $40,000 that I could have used to buy a house, go on trips, hire a cook, buy a car . . . or make four albums . . .

After graduating, instead of pursuing musical endeavours, I got a job as a barista while I tried to sort myself out. I remember feeling degraded serving my peers and instructors coffee and taking out the smelly garbage in front of them as they discussed their current exciting creative projects. I worked as a barista for almost four years, with little income and even less direction. Even though my musical instruction was rich and wonderful, I did not receive the tools I needed for overcoming the barriers and limitations in my own mind that prevented me from moving forward. When I look back now at my time in university, I consider it to be one of the biggest regrets of my life. Not because I wish I was an opera singer, but because I let fear sit on the throne in my mind for all of those years. I missed out on so many fun, collaborative experiences and musical connections. I try not to spend too much time thinking about that because it brings me to a melancholic place that I can't pull up from easily. Moving on.

As funny as it sounds, the two people who influenced me to overcome my singing hermitude were Judy Garland and Mickey Rooney. In their four big-screen Hollywood musicals together from the 1940s, the same story unfolds in different situations. Their characters are rejected by the music business, they despair, and then something arises inside them that makes them say, "Don't quit!" They decide to create their own show, despite the opposition, and end up succeeding in achieving their dreams. As silly as this sounds, watching these old cheese-bally musicals influenced me to take action and put on my own little show. A dancer friend and I put together our own evening of musical theatre, raising over $10,000 for charity. I learned dance routines for the first time in my life, and we performed Fred and Judy's "A Couple of Swells" from the musical *Easter Parade* close to perfection. Because of the success of that night, I decided to audition for two musicals, and I got a part in one of them. Being cast in that show led me to another job singing classical soprano in Mozart's "Vesperae solennes de confessore." I was slowly coming out of hiding and taking chances. Almost nothing in the artistic world can be achieved without risk. But we will talk more about that later.

At twenty-seven, I auditioned to be on a music team that I really wanted to be a part of in a large church. Unfortunately, I was still an operatic soprano and not at all the modern style they were looking for. I was told very kindly by the director that I should take singing lessons from his wife. OMG. Can you imagine? That moment is etched firmly into my memory bank and felt like a sharp blade sunk deep into my chest. After all, I had a vocal music degree and what seemed like a zillion years of singing lessons under my belt. Had he said something like, "Hey, you sound great, but we are looking for singers who have this type of singing background," it might not have crushed me as hard. But you don't often get rejection in a neat little care package. Hearing him say, "You should take singing lessons from my wife," was so hard for me to process because my mind took that and made up thousands of reasons why he didn't like me and why I wasn't good enough. This led me to believe my very essence wasn't good enough. I allowed one small moment to become a soul-crushing one. Rejection, specific or not, can be devastating if we aren't settled in ourselves first.

Because I believed my worth as a singer was in other people's words and opinions, something that was sincerely meant to help me knocked me out of commission. I completely stopped singing at this point, believing the lie that my voice just wasn't ever going to be good enough and I was a complete and total failure as a singer. I am talking the most ginormous world-class pity party. At least I could be the best at something—having pity parties—and I invited the whole block. I didn't even sing in church from the pews anymore because I believed my voice wasn't good enough.

How. Utterly. Ridiculous. Because I had no mental fortitude or training, the pain was raw and real and didn't subside very easily.

After six months of wallowing, self-loathing, and wasting time, something finally rose up in me and said, "I am going to prove him wrong." I began a ten-year learning journey where I learned to play all the instruments in a band decently, learned intermediate-level music production, learned about gear and how a sound system works, studied jazz theory with a local jazz musician, worked on developing modern singing techniques, and began pushing really hard to better myself. I also invested money to work with singers and producers who were ahead of me skill-wise.

I got a job with Yamaha teaching music and working with young adults. I began as a vocal coach, instructing standard material, but as I have evolved over the last decade to who I am today with my own studio, I am now much more of a 'whole musician:' singer/songwriter/coach. I love teaching singers how to create and play music for themselves and how to produce and put a track together. Teaching also helped me find my way. Ninety percent of my students came into my studio too afraid to perform or sing for anyone. They were content to sing in their bedrooms or under the stairs in their basements *wink* for the rest of their lives. As someone who was no longer afraid and was in the process of defeating the majority of my fears, it irked me to see some of my students living within the same dark cave that I had lived in for so long. I began working with those ones, teaching them how to overcome fear, because I deeply understood what it could do to the life of a creative. When you overcome something in your personal life, you can easily give your success away to someone else so they can get there faster. This is what I want to give away to you in this book. The ability to see and recognize every obstacle in front of your artistic path as something that can be knocked down and moved aside. If you are willing to put effort in, you can win. If you don't quit, you win. Let me say that again—**If you don't quit, you win.**

CHAPTER 2

CHANGING FALSE BELIEF SYSTEMS

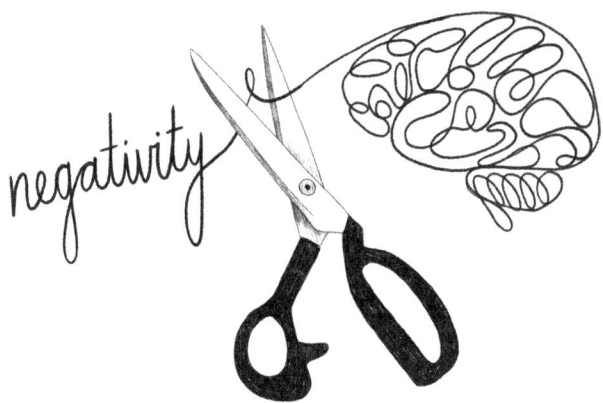

Okay, everybody, buckle up because we are going to dive deep right away in this chapter. Are you ready? My students know that I am a very direct person who sometimes forgets to say hello at the beginning of my texts and lessons because I am so excited about all the things we are going to accomplish that day. So . . . hello. Lol.

I want to start out by giving you an important foundational concept that will apply to every single part of the rest of this book. The concept is this: **what you believe, you will live out**. If you are taking notes, write that down. Think about that for a second before reading on. You will live out what you believe about yourself and your art form. For example, if you believed you were a terrible painter, you probably wouldn't be showing anyone your work, or even enjoy creating it anymore. You would live inside the world your belief system created, which is that you are an awful painter, and probably avoid painting entirely. Your behaviour (avoiding painting) would only be a symptom of the belief that was rooted deep in your mind and heart.

If you believe negative things about yourself or your art, that is going to **directly impact** your journey as a creative. Your art comes out of who you are and is a reflection of you, so how you feel about yourself unequivocally influences it and can be one of the main reasons behind blocked creativity. I interact with young creators who are too afraid to take a step, showcase their art, and share their gift and who have stalled in their creative journey. The mental block almost always comes from a faulty belief system. If you believe you are never going to make it, will you ever try? Why would you try to make it if you believe that you won't? **Your belief system influences your actions**. Are you getting the point I am trying to make here? A rule in my studio is to never speak negatively about your gift because the more a student says, "My voice sounds so awful," the more they shrink back into silence. I do, however, believe in speaking truthful, constructive things like, "I didn't get that right," or "That didn't sound so good yet." If you are looking to grow in skill, feedback is such a necessary and positive thing. The difference? Constructive criticism will be rooted in truth, and a negative belief system will usually be rooted in a lie. Giving your art a factual and helpful critique is way different than saying, "That was disgusting," or "I am a terrible singer."

It is absolutely essential that you keep an eye out for these sneaky little false beliefs that stay tucked away, hidden in the corners within the windmills of your mind. They are of no use to you and are likely negatively influencing you without you even knowing it. Sometimes even pessimistic thoughts about yourself that seem totally disconnected from your art form still have a huge influence over it. For example, I have had more than one student spend hours every morning doing their makeup before school. One student would set her alarm for 4 a.m. on a school day because she didn't want anyone to see her as she was. Some of you might think that something like this wouldn't necessarily affect her artistic journey, but it affected EVERY part of it and also every other part of her day because she was getting so little sleep. She was a skilled musician, a great singer who played multiple instruments, and had a bold personality, but she was petrified of sharing anything musical on the internet or social media. Her beautiful original song that I helped record and produce was hidden away, just like her face. She would go through a four-hour rehearsal without saying a word to any of her peers. I can't even tell you the many ways that insecurity affected her music. The majority of people she knew pronounced her name wrong, which she hated, but she never corrected them and settled for being called the wrong name. Do you see the problem here? This extremely smart and talented student's main dream in life was to become a singer and release her own music, but because of the negative things she believed about herself, she was immobilized and concealed. She was like a stuck chess piece, unable to make a move, checked by fear. How she viewed herself influenced her art, her ability to share her art, her art's authenticity, and her entire life.

The assignment I give students with a really negative belief system is two-fold. Firstly, I like to find and identify the false mindset behind the problematic behaviour. That allows us to name our foe and begin to work through some of the thoughts and actions that have been controlled by it. Secondly, I assign them something intentional to do in order to combat that belief in their daily lives. With this particular student, we discovered many lies she believed about herself, her appearance, and her weight, and we began writing them all down. Beside the negatives, we wrote down truthful statements or affirmations that we wanted to replace them with. I asked her to look in the mirror and read out the affirmations we had made every day for thirty days. As well as doing that, I asked her to do a two-week makeup fast, something practical to do in the real world to go alongside the affirmations. The resistance and panic in her when I presented this idea was so intense. She almost couldn't do it. The fear of letting other people see her as she was, was crippling. (Disclaimer: this girl is gorgeous.) We texted back and forth the night before as she was trying to turn off the fear that was screaming at her in her mind. It was a real battle.

It was not easy, but she did it. After a week or two of hanging her head low in school in embarrassment, she realized that no one cared whether she wore makeup or not. After two weeks, I told her she could wear makeup again but was only allowed to spend fifteen minutes a day on it—not four hours. After a month, she shared with me how much better her days were with the right amount of sleep each night, and she even began to find the thought of setting a four o'clock alarm to do her makeup for a math class ridiculous. She is still working toward being completely comfortable in her own skin, but this was a major step in the right direction, and I am so proud of her. I can't wait to hear what she comes up with musically in the next season of her life. She started correcting people when they pronounced her name wrong, and as I am writing this, she has started working on two original songs with me.

If you want to share your art with the world, hiding is out of the question. If your goal is to be influential, look for the false beliefs that keep you concealed, and then begin the work to change them. It is possible! It is not pride to love who you are. I live in Manitoba now where I teach a lot of teenagers who, because of their faith environment, sometimes hold on to the strange belief that they have to put themselves down and appear less gifted in order to demonstrate humility. Hogwash, I say! Making yourself shine less does not make you humble or make your Creator happy.

> *"Changing your inner script is a process. Changing it doesn't happen overnight because usually those beliefs got chiselled into your mind and your being over time. I think that changing your inner script is a daily practice. It is as simple as looking in the mirror and saying things like 'I have beautiful eyes,' or 'I am a great friend.' I think it is about having some time every day where you talk about the things that you love about yourself. The qualities that you love, that you are proud of. It's about learning to be really generous with yourself. That is a process, and it is a daily practice. The other side of that is that as soon as those negative thoughts come in, you stop them. When you have a negative thought about yourself, stop it right away, and speak out the positive. Even if you don't believe it yet."*

Shoshana Bean – Singer, Songwriter, Recording Artist, Broadway Veteran [1]

When I first met Natasha, I saw so much beauty and potential in her warm voice and in her heartfelt creativity. The only problem was we couldn't get through a music lesson without her insulting herself and telling me how absolutely disgusting her voice was and how terrible her original songs were. That happened every two minutes for the whole hour. Because I do not allow students to insult themselves in lessons, I stopped her. Every. Single. Time. And I had her speak out a more truthful fact about the situation. Instead of "My voice is disgusting," I would have her say, "I am learning to train my voice. My voice is improving." Lessons with Tash started out very slowly because we had to keep stopping to address the negative words being spoken. I am actually surprised she did not quit in her first six months with me as I was so strict with her, and we got so little music done. Here is her story in her own words.

Natasha's Story:

"We do not realize this a lot of the time, but negativity is such a strong force and can hold us back from so much if we let it. I struggled a lot with negative thoughts toward myself, and it had such an impact on my music. I love music and singing. I have sung since I was little, and music has always been in my life. At one point I started taking voice lessons from an opera singer, but I only ever sang for her because I was too scared to sing for others, even my own family. I was terrified to sing for someone and mess up and disappoint them. I was afraid someone would tell me that what I believed was true, that I wasn't good enough to sing. One day I was auditioning for a play in front of my school. The teacher wanted to hear us sing individually, and I was nervous and scared that I would mess up. When it was my turn, it did not go well, and I sang way too high. It was so embarrassing. Everyone was watching and heard me. In my mind, I had failed because I knew I could have sung better and wanted so badly to prove that to others. Long story short, I didn't get a main part, which I took as confirmation that I wasn't good enough. Being surrounded by some unhealthy friends, my fears and negativity only grew, and negativity became my defence mechanism. I thought that if I could insult my voice before anyone else did, I could stop myself from getting hurt by others.

I was so afraid of what people would think or say, I insulted myself even when I thought I had sung well.

"My negativity came out of my fear of what others would think or say, along with my desire to do things well. Something Heidi has taught me that changed my view on everything is that singing, or whatever art you do, isn't about what others are thinking or about how 'talented' you are; it is about giving what you have away. We all contribute in different ways, have different styles, different voices, and different gifts. When you sing, it is more important to sing from the heart than to impress people. You will always make mistakes, especially at first, but making mistakes doesn't determine how talented you are. Don't let negativity suck the life out of what you love, hold you back from your potential, or keep you from sharing your talent with others. Words hold so much power, so don't let negative ones settle over you. It might be frustrating at first or seem useless, but taking a second to cut off those thoughts and replace them with something positive or constructive can make such a big difference. I started in my craft not being able to get through a song without stopping and criticizing myself. Now I can record a video of me singing a song multiple times, push through the mistakes, send a good take in to Heidi, and share my bloopers. I am even singing solos in school and church now. In the end, it is up to you—no matter how long you have been doing what you are doing and how much training you have or haven't gotten—whether thousands will get to experience what you have to offer or if no one will. If you don't learn to shut off the negativity, you will only get so far. So, take a breath, silence your thoughts, and give yourself grace. **All you can give is what you have, and believe that what you have is something worth giving.**"

Natasha was asked to lead one of her school's music teams and was given the part of Jo March in her school's production of *Little Women*. She has become a safe place for new singers, has written multiple songs, and sang for PTP faithfully. There were also a couple of times this last while where things really fell apart on stage with her band, like the power going out one morning during her set. She didn't flinch. In fact, she told me, laughing, about what a disaster one of the mornings she had sung was. Because her belief system about herself has changed, one failure doesn't touch her identity anymore, and she can keep learning and growing her skills.

If you are a creative, most likely, the internal work will never stop. Even now as I just turned forty, sneaky little beliefs still pop up for me that I didn't realize were there. I can choose to shove them down and stall or allow them to surface and move past them.

Something else that will really benefit you is taking a moment to speak positive words out loud over yourself. I am going to leave space for this at the end of each chapter. We will call them 'Mindful Meditations.' Take a moment and read them out loud. Try to say them from your heart instead of your mind because your heart is where the change begins . . . when it comes into agreement. Think about the words of the meditation you are saying with the intention to embrace its truth. You may need to say a sentence several times before you really feel your heart grabbing onto it and making it your own. Some of the meditations might be hard to speak aloud, so you might just be saying them out of self-discipline at first. You may need to repeat the meditation three times for it to sink in, or it may take you thirty. Don't give up! It can take a bit of time for your heart to come into agreement with these new beliefs. Maybe start by choosing one that really resonates with you, and then do this exercise with it for a month.

Also, feel free to personalize or alter any of the meditations to suit your personal journey, but try to stay with the theme of the chapter. It may also help to have music in the background to keep you relaxed and calm. Take three to five deep breaths from the diaphragm at the beginning, in the middle, and at the end as you take in, so to speak, the words of meditation. Ready? Here we go . . .

MINDFUL MEDITATION:

"I choose to release the pattern of negative thoughts that no longer serves me in a positive way. I am worthwhile. I am worthwhile. I am worthwhile. I am grateful for my journey as an artist. I have all that I need to express what is in me to express. My artistic expression is beautiful and beneficial to others. It is valuable. I am valuable. I am appreciated, and I appreciate myself. I love who I am."

CHAPTER SUMMARY:

- What you believe about yourself and your craft will influence its direction.
- You can change belief systems with effort.
- Choose what you believe about yourself and your art carefully.
- Avoid speaking harmful negative words over your gift. Constructive factual criticism is okay, though.

QUESTIONS TO PONDER:

1) What percentage of my thoughts are positive about my art, and what percentage are negative?
2) How often do I insult my abilities?
3) What are some negative beliefs I hold about myself that are due for a change?

NOTES:

CHAPTER 3
HAVING THE RIGHT MOTIVATION

"I feel most in my element when dancing. Like my mind, body, and spirit are all actually connected and working together as one. When dancing becomes hard, I don't feel immediately frustrated or disheartened. Instead, I enjoy the chase and challenge of mentally and physically getting better. I am also so drawn to the sense of community that I receive from dance. It holds the types of relationships and way of relating to people that I value."

Emily Solstice Tait – Dancer

I am drawn to artists and influencers who are authentic, who can post selfies without layers of makeup on, who can laugh at themselves when they fail, and who are not afraid to advertise their own shortcomings. Artists like this are fresh air to me. When I see a singer, dancer, performer, or actor who is trying hard to impress me with how 'good' they are, I walk away. I don't mind being impressed by someone's skill, (in fact, I really love it), but if I can see that impressing me is their primary motivation, I am not interested. Here's the nugget: Your reason for what you do should be **to share your art and influence people with it**, to communicate something that is inside you through whatever art form you partake in. You might end up being impressive, but having 'impressing' be your primary motivator means that your art is all about status when it should be about your audience and what you are trying to communicate.

> *"The mindset of getting out of your own ego and being about giving as opposed to getting has changed my life and my career path. Make it not about yourself, make it about something bigger and outside of yourself. You have nothing to prove, only to share."*
>
> **Shoshana Bean** [2]

In the music world, I look at the singers who have the attitude of 'worship at my altar and see how amazing I am' and cringe. When you follow and idolize someone like that, the **pressure to become someone impressive and larger than life** gets planted inside you. Then when you fail to become 'larger than life,' you become upset with yourself and head down a rabbit hole of depression. My personal code is that who I am onstage or in the public eye should be the same as who I am offstage. Even if you are an actor, you want to portray your character using elements of yourself and your past experiences to bring emotion and authenticity to the role.

> *"The purpose of art is washing the dust of daily life off our souls."*
>
> **Pablo Picasso** [3]

"The purpose of art is to raise people to a higher level of awareness than they would otherwise attain on their own."

Brassaï [4]

"The purpose of art is nothing less than the upliftment of the human spirit."

Pope John Paul II [5]

If impressing people and gaining followers is my only motivation, what does that say about me? How shallow does that make my art? My students know I am a straight shooter when it comes to these things. I say the hard things, but it's because I want them—and you—to succeed. Impressing people and gaining status cannot be your primary motivators.

Impressing people actually causes more stress when you showcase your work because you really don't know if the people you are trying to impress will be! So you come in uncertain, like with a job interview or a blind date, asking yourself things like: Will they like me? Won't they? Am I enough? Am I not enough? **The only thing you can control is making your art honestly, to the best of your abilities, and then sharing it.** If you go in with the attitude of giving something away, then there is no pressure. I can't control whether my mom will like her Christmas gift in the same way I can't control whether someone will like my latest song. All I can control is my sincere motivation in picking it out for her and giving it to her. If you are giving the audience a gift, you are sharing, not impressing.

"Creativity isn't about our genius. It's about our generosity."

Ray Hughes – Author, Storyteller, Composer of over one thousand songs

If we look a little deeper at someone living for applause and affirmation, they are often insecure and striving to gain value by getting the approval of other people. Examples of false beliefs here would be: "I am worthy if other people say I am" or "I will matter if I get enough followers on Instagram." There is nothing wrong with wanting positive feedback from other people, but I don't recommend living for it. I believe you need to look inward or upward for those kinds of affirmations. The work to change your motivation might seem gruelling, but the result is that your entire playing field changes, your entire reason for doing what you do shifts, and your art becomes purer. Everything changes. I remember the moment this sunk in for me and have everlasting gratitude for it. It felt like my eyes suddenly came into focus, and I could see clearly for the first time. I had sung to impress and obtain value for SO long, and I had been fearful and stressed every time I performed. Letting that stress go was one of the best things that ever happened to me.

> *"All throughout life, we are going to be promoted, and we're going to be demoted. It's the circle of life that crafts our character. Be the same person when nobody is looking. Because that's the reality of who you are. It's a beautiful thing."*
>
> **Julie Meyer – Singer-Songwriter, Recording Artist, Author, Speaker**

Sometimes I can see a young musician from afar and know exactly what they need from me in order for them to succeed. When I first met Solomon, I saw someone with incredible talent musically but lacking authenticity and the right motivations for his craft. I was delighted when he approached me for a vocal lesson.

Solomon's Story:

"I've loved music ever since I was a little boy, grabbing sticks and beating on rocks as if they were drums. When I was twelve years old, my mom told me that the church was looking for a drummer, and they were wondering if I'd be willing to learn. This is where my life changed, and I began my journey as an artist. I became obsessed with drumming so much that I built my own drums because my father didn't want to buy me a kit. He said it would make too much noise, and he wouldn't be able to sleep. A few months later, after practicing day and night, the church chose another person to drum instead of me. When I heard this, I felt all my dreams shattering, and I swore I would never do music again. But my mother didn't allow me to give up on myself that easily. She said, 'Well, the church needs a guitarist, so maybe that's what you want.' The same immediate intense passion and drive overwhelmed me again, and at age thirteen, I started to learn the guitar.

"I was always somebody who fell in love easily. At age fourteen, I had my first girlfriend, and she inspired me to write my first love songs. I wrote so many songs and learned how to play so well that by age sixteen, I became the most skilled musician in my church.

"Without me noticing, ego began creeping in because I had finally found something I was good at. There is good pride and there is bad pride. Being proud of your work and accomplishments is a good thing. Feeling superior to other people is not. I had been bullied when I was younger and even though I was at the top of the game in my circle, I think deep down I still felt inferior, which manifested in me as ego and superiority toward others. The scary part about it was that I had no idea that my self-conceit was getting out of control in me.

"No one in church ever called me on it. Maybe that was because I was the pastor's son, and they were scared to correct me about anything.

"At age seventeen, I left my home country of Belize to come to Canada to pursue music. I was so determined to accomplish my dreams and be recognized as an artist worldwide that I worked almost non-stop on my music career. I wrote songs, I produced them, I entered contests, and I did whatever it took to get my name out there.

"Along the way I met my first vocal instructor, Heidi Korte. Up until that moment, everyone had always told me how talented I was. Heidi did not. She gave me constructive criticism on our first lesson and told me I needed help with some muscles I was tensing in my throat when I sang. This completely offended me because no one had ever told me I needed help with anything musical before.

"I had a few sessions with her, and looking back, she was truly the mentor who initiated my journey of finding authenticity in myself and my music. I've always felt like I had to fight other people for what I wanted, but Heidi taught me how to let go and just be myself. I recognize now that my pride stemmed from the insecurity I felt as a young boy with no purpose and no talent.

"My advice for overcoming ego:

1) Remove the spotlight from yourself.

2) Make your craft about other people.

3) Find gratitude in every little thing.

4) Speak positively about the people you dislike.

5) Start to help the people around you achieve their dreams.

Doing all this is who we are meant to be.
Love Solomon." (@Skyzzmusic)

In one of my favourite CBC interviews with music legend Johnny Cash, Cash shares humbly about why he thinks people connect so much with his music. The first thing he says is that there is something beyond having just technical skill and that's emotional connection. Take a moment to think about that. How much of your time is devoted to skill alone in your field? There is something magical that lies beyond skill that I hope all of you will run towards after reading this book. Another reason he gives is that he loves what he does and that comes out in his work and people are drawn in by that. (But don't take my word for it, find the interview and hear it directly from the master.[6])

If I am honest with you, this 'what is my motivation' thing is still a work in progress for me. I spent thirty-three years singing to impress people, and at forty, I have to stop, close my eyes, and remind myself out loud before I step on stage or start filming a music video, "Love your audience, Heidi. Sing to give, not to get." I believe this will eventually become second nature for me, but right now both my brain and heart still need the reminder.

I remember the first house concert I ever did. My good friend Brigid put it on for me and did all the advertising. I was so scared. I remember hiding down in her basement doing my vocal warmups, petrified of talking to people before the show, of how the performance was going to go, of letting the ticket payers down, and of showing weakness. I sang that evening just as I had practiced and the audience was so unbelievably warm, loving, and accepting of me. I can actually still see their smiling faces in my mind. I would love to do that night over and include them and actually sing 'for them.' I was so focused on impressing them with my talent and not making any mistakes that I actually missed out on enjoying the evening with them.

The fear of disappointing me used to be the primary motivator for one of my extremely talented students. It was actually difficult to unearth as on the outside, Damian appeared to be highly committed, always arriving prepared for his lesson. I knew he struggled with anxiety, but it took a while for me to realize that fear was his sole motivator for music. Here is his story in his own words.

Damian's Story:

"When I started music lessons in grade seven, my thoughts went something like this: 'whatever I do is wrong,' and 'people will never be impressed with me.' If people didn't like what I played or how I played, and if I couldn't play it perfectly, then I wasn't good enough. Each week coming to lessons, I feared that Heidi would judge me and tell me I sucked. Those were the normal Damian thoughts—always have to be perfect. When I practiced at home, I felt like I was only doing it because I was scared, and I needed to please Heidi so that she wouldn't be mad at me. That belief I held to is what drove me to practice really hard every week.

"Heidi finally asked me one day if that was why I was practicing so hard, and I admitted it was. She told me that I was no longer allowed to practice while I was afraid. She told me to take a minute to calm my brain down and that if I couldn't calm it down, I was to skip practicing that day. She even said that she wouldn't be disappointed if I skipped the whole week. She didn't want my music to be linked with fear anymore. Another belief I had was that other people got things right immediately, and I was the only who got it wrong when I practiced.

"Today, I like my voice. I hated my voice before. I like singing on stage now and am more peaceful performing knowing that I am presenting my voice as a gift to my audience. It's not up to me whether or not they love it. I am only in control of what I am in control of. It also helps knowing that there are people in my life that love me and care for me when I make mistakes. When you're vulnerable and authentic, people love you more. They can relate with you more. They don't think of you less, they are drawn to you more."

The great singer and actress Lena Horne told Rosie O'Donnell in an interview that the first time she liked singing wasn't until age fifty when she finally realized that the audience wanted her to connect with them through her singing.[7] I look at her career and how many albums she'd made and movies she had been in before age fifty, and that blows my mind. This realization came to me personally at thirty-three. I had, up until then, always tried to impress my audience with skill alone and had actually spent my first teaching years training my students to do the same. I will forever be grateful for the moment I realized I had gotten it wrong. It's not when you learn it, it's gratitude for the fact that you get to learn it at all.

MINDFUL MEDITATION:

> "I give and receive without expectation. I create from an abundant heart. Love is my centre. I share my art to bring joy and inspiration to others. I choose to give freely."

CHAPTER SUMMARY:

- The purpose of art is to share or communicate something.
- Trying to impress will only cause stress and anxiety to surface.
- Art is about giving, not getting.

QUESTIONS TO PONDER:

1) Why am I making art?
2) Is my art a true reflection of me and my imagination?
3) Am I creating to give or to get? Am I performing to give or to get?

NOTES:

_____

_____

_____

_____

_____

_____

_____

CHAPTER 4
IDENTITY AND SELF-WORTH

As artists, it is essential that we learn to separate who we are from what we do. In general, that's a healthy thing for everyone to do, but especially for creatives. This separation is necessary for maintaining mental health because as I mentioned earlier, what we create is graded by other people, audition panels, reviews, or even by view count. I remember getting my first dislike on a YouTube video and being so gutted. Then I investigated some of my favourite performers' YouTube channels, and I saw how many dislikes they had and somehow that made me feel better. If you are afraid to share your creations for fear of other people hating them, I would ask you if you like all the different genres in music. Blues? Metal? Jazz? Latin? Probably not. Is it okay that you don't like a particular genre? Yes, it is. It is also okay if not everyone is drawn to your art. It really is. I don't like every style that's out there and can't expect all people to fall in love with my style. Some people will love what you do, others may hate it. Your self-worth cannot be in people's response to your art. If it is, your emotional stability will be a rickety rollercoaster. You'll be on top of the world when your song hits one hundred thousand streams, but at the bottom emotionally when your next project flops. Is it okay to celebrate if your play is doing well or your short film is getting good reviews? Yes, absolutely. But where it becomes unhealthy is when your self-worth depends on getting good feedback and reviews. As an artist, sometimes things will not go well, and you need to be okay with yourself after a bad show or review. That doesn't mean you do a sloppy job or set out to have things go wrong either. You must always do your absolute best and show up as prepared as you can. But when words are forgotten, the power goes out, or allergies make your high notes crack, you need to be able to laugh it off and keep moving forward.

I read the book *From Spiritual Slavery to Spiritual Sonship* by Jack Frost in my twenties, and in his and his wife Trisha's teachings, an analogy about icebergs really stuck with me.[8] So much so that this is the main way I describe identity and self-esteem to my students.

An iceberg has just a small portion that rests above the water while the majority of it, ninety percent, is hidden beneath the water. We are going to label the little part above the water as the part of you that can be seen by others: your performance, your gift, or your product. The ninety percent of you that is underneath the water is who you are apart from your gifting: your personality, beliefs, likes and dislikes, quirks, and all the things that can't be seen by others. When a storm, or say the Titanic, hits an iceberg, that tiny bit above the water takes the damage, while the massive bottom part underneath is left intact. Using our gifting analogy, when your self-worth is in your product (that top part of the iceberg), as soon as a storm comes (a negative review or rejection) your self-esteem gets obliterated. The majority of your self-worth has to be in who you are as a person, the unseen part. **We are human beings, not just human doings.** If your self-esteem is tangled up with your result, then most likely, your confidence and emotions will be constantly changing based on 'how well' you are doing at that particular moment instead of being secure in who you are as a human. In the future, you will have great reviews, bad reviews, fall in a dance, and maybe do a triple pirouette successfully. In each of those things, though, you need to be okay with who you are, comfortable in both failure and success. Failure doesn't define you, and neither does success. If your art doesn't become globally famous, you are enough. Let me say that again because you might not believe me. **Who you are—with or without your art—is enough.**

Take a minute before reading on to practice mindfulness. This book is really about **how you respond to some of these concepts.** It's not reading to the end that will magically transform you, it is these moments right here. It's the process. Close your eyes and think of things aside from your art that you value about yourself. Breathe deeply and allow love for who you are, your personality, and even your physical body to surface. Allow gratitude for your life to surface. And just sit in this emotion of contentment. Loving yourself is a choice, and in this moment, I'd like you to choose to love yourself.

For my student Rogan, the subject of identity didn't surface until our second or third year of lessons. We spent the majority of our time together focused on the business of growing him in piano and teaching him how to write and produce music, that it wasn't until much later we discovered his "why" needed some realigning.

Rogan's Story:

"I joined my church's youth band at the age of twelve when I didn't know how to play. I started taking lessons, and I would have to say that pretty quickly, I surpassed the other pianists in the youth band in terms of knowledge and ability. This started thoughts in me like, 'I'm better than them,' or 'The leaders put me in for this day because they know I am more talented.' Or if I wasn't playing one morning, I would listen offstage for the times where I could have played better than the piano player on stage.

"There were many times where I'd be playing a set with the band and I'd think to myself, 'I have skill, so I should show off how good I am,' or when someone new would walk into the room, I would think, 'I just need to show off how good I am at playing scales.' Using what you've learned in lessons in the real world isn't a bad thing; in fact, it's the whole point. The problem with me was that I was doing it to show off. I'd learned all these skills in music class, which was good, but then I felt that because I could play better than the other pianists, I should always make sure to play better than them. I created very high standards for myself because my self-worth was in how good I played. It was like I was trying desperately to prove that I mattered to other musicians and listeners. My playing started to feel mechanical and pretty soon, I realized that I didn't enjoy being on stage very much anymore. I enjoyed playing more when I just let myself feel the music and got into its groove.

"I think the most important thing is that you're really feeling what you are doing. Are you having fun on the stage? I believed the lies that if I didn't play well enough, the audience wouldn't enjoy our band, or if I wasn't playing to my full potential, then people wouldn't be engaged by our music. In reality, it was much the opposite.

"Now I try to feel what I am doing instead of thinking about how others are viewing me, and I don't judge myself when I mess up. If you mess up and look like a fool, awesome! We learn from mistakes.

"Sometimes thoughts still come into my mind about trying to play to impress and show off, but when they do, I just push them aside and remind myself that I'm not playing to impress, rather to have fun, try new things, and feel new things. Play to grow, not to impress."

I read a post written by my friend Charles on Instagram that arrested my attention and sent me on a thought journey. I would encourage you all to stop and discover the beauty and truth of this for yourselves.

> *"Your gift is valuable, no doubt about it. However, your gift only has value because you have your hands on it. Your gift literally doesn't mean anything unless you're attached to it. Example: Have you ever noticed how useless a mirror is until you stand in front of it? It's because mirrors don't have an identity of their own, so they need identity to stand in front of them in order to be used. It's the same thing with gifts . . . There are a million singers in the world, but there's only one you. A million painters, but only one you . . . A million poets, but only one you.* **You give identity to your gift, not the other way around***."*
>
> *Charles Patton II – Red Lion @redlionpoetry*

I could sit and get lost inside that thought all day. I have never heard it worded more beautifully. Now remember—don't panic when you discover something in your thinking that needs work. It's actually such a blessing when I find a part of me that needs realigning. It means there is more breathing room on the other side of things, and I am grateful that the problem was brought to my attention. It doesn't mean you are 'troubled' or 'need a lot of work' if you have these issues, it just means there is room for further growth and expansion!

MINDFUL MEDITATION:

> "I am worthy and loved apart from my artistic expression. I let go of self-criticism. I open my heart to receive acceptance from myself and others. I approve of myself. My artistic expression does not define me. I am complete as I am."

CHAPTER SUMMARY:

- Your identity should be who you are, not what you do.
- Your gift is a reflection of your identity.

QUESTIONS TO PONDER:

1) How do I handle bad reviews, bad performances?
2) Does my self-esteem fluctuate depending on how well I do, or is it steady?
3) Is there anything that needs realigning in this area? Take a moment to practice this by visualizing a recent failure. Picture yourself in that moment, and show grace to yourself. Love yourself in that moment. Breathe.

NOTES:

_____
_____
_____
_____
_____
_____

CHAPTER 5

FEAR

Fear. You again. Fear and anxiety are what I almost always encounter whenever I take on a new student. So many of them are unwilling to perform, unwilling to let their parents and family hear them practice, unwilling to post any singing videos, and some cry singing in front of me for the first while or even the first year (xoxo). I personally think that those ones are meant to be with me for that very reason, as I love seeing them become confident. If your art form requires you to be in the public eye, you will need to develop some level of confidence!

I have walked through deep waters with many young singers that needed help sorting through fear. One student Angelina stands out in particular. She LOVED singing, loved music, loved dancing, and had a vibrant, funny, engaging personality. I looked at her and said, "Ange, you need to be entertaining people, you are hilarious!" She could imitate voices and accents, and she moved so well on the dance floor. In singing lessons, however, she was crippled by an extreme fear that all notes were too high for her. She would crank the volume up on my piano so loud that I could not hear anything she sang in a lesson. She was freakishly stubborn and refused to turn it down when I asked, which was . . . a delight. Angelina was a great drummer in my younger student band, but she quit because she was too afraid to talk to her bandmates in rehearsals. Finally, one day in grade seven or eight, she said to me, "Heidi, I am scared all the time. When I am scared, I smile, and by the end of the day, my face hurts from smiling so hard." That got me thinking about how I could help her overcome fear in music and maybe also in life. I came up with a plan for her to take fifty small healthy risks by the end of the school year to slowly start chipping away at fear. It was an experiment to see if we could intentionally grow some confidence in her. She was too young for me to talk about false beliefs with, and I know that kind of conversation would have overwhelmed her at the time. So instead, we made a risk list, and every time she did something scary that was good for her, she would write the date and the risk. The list of her fears was long. Well, she not only took fifty risks, she took one hundred that first year! And the next year she did at least fifty. Once a risk wasn't frightening anymore, it no longer counted as a risk. This approach worked so well with Ange that I began using it with almost every new student coming into my studio that struggled with fear so that they could actively do something to chip away at fear during their week. **Fear has no business being a part of the creative's mindset**. Sit with that for a minute. I remember the day Ange started singing at her high school in the stairwell on her lunch break. She did that regularly during her last year there. On top of that, she started to post singing videos on her own YouTube channel, and even got signed with a modelling agency. Fear does not hold her back anymore, and that just makes me bubble-over-happy on the inside. Here is Angelina's story in her own words.

Angelina's Story:

"This year I graduated high school, and as I walked out of the school for the last time, my grade nine math teacher approached me and said something that I've thought about ever since. He said, 'Angelina, it is so amazing to see who you've become in these past four years. I remember you in grade nine being one of the shyest kids in my class, and now I look at you and you are so confident and so sure of yourself.' He went on about how he'd seen me grow into the person I am today. In that moment I reflected on who I used to be, who I am now, and how much I've truly changed, not only in the past four years of high school but since I was really young. When I was a child, just about everything scared me, including singing in front of people, taking the bus, crossing the street, riding my bike, writing music, drumming in a band, talking to people, and going to school. The first time I had to take a public bus to school, I forced my mom to take it with me because I was scared to get off at the wrong stop. Funny thing is, it was more embarrassing having my mom ride the bus with me when there were mainly just kids on it. I remember I dropped out of dancing classes because I was so nervous about how everyone would see me and what they would think about me. Dancing, to this day, is one of my favourite things, and I didn't stay in it because I was too afraid. I also dropped out of drum lessons for the same reason. I turned down so many fun and amazing opportunities because I was too scared to do them. Singing recitals were one of the worst things in my life. I was so nervous about them that I'd make Heidi over-prepare me, and I would sing my recital song every day three months ahead of time. I was also very quick to give up and say I couldn't do things because I was afraid of not getting it right and that Heidi would think I was stupid. Later on, I discovered that most things in music came easy to me once I stopped being afraid. Heidi would never let me get away with saying I couldn't do something. She would stop me every single time and say, 'YET, Ange. You can't do this YET.' She would make me repeat it, which, in the moment, was annoying. With time though, I stopped saying 'I can't,' and the less I said it, the less I believed it. We also made a risk page, and whenever I did something that scared me, I'd get a check mark, and after it was full,

I'd get something for it. I started taking a lot of small risks because of that list.

"So how did I go from not being able to talk to anyone to being able to do anything I wanted without fear? A lot of work. It took years of retraining my mind to finally understand how fear works, because at the end of the day, fear is just a little voice in your head telling you that you shouldn't do something, telling you that you can't do something. Fear is something to be overcome, especially in someone who allows fear to control their whole life, like I did. Don't get me wrong, to this day, I still get anxious about certain things, everyone does, and that's okay! The difference is that even though I'm nervous about that job interview, it doesn't mean I'm not going to go and do it with confidence. The old me would have never done something like that, and that's where my growth is so noticeable to my parents, my friends, and even my grade nine math teacher. Self-love is another amazing thing that helps with fear. Being yourself and putting your true self out there is absolutely the best thing. Overcoming fear is about being confident and knowing that even if you do mess up . . . WHO CARES? No one! You just get up and try again, and you move on. There is absolutely nothing wrong with making a mistake. In fact, mistakes are just lessons, and they are good, healthy things that everyone has to go through all the time. Don't hold yourself back because you are afraid of messing up or afraid that you can't do it. Those voices in your head . . . ignore them, and prove them wrong. Do whatever makes you happy, and never stop being yourself. Remember that fear doesn't control you—you control your fear. Don't let a tiny, small thing like fear stop you from doing what you love!"

I think because of working with Angelina, newer students like Ambria coming into the studio get the chance to work through it at a faster pace. Somehow seeing the success and struggle of those before them gives them extra gumption and courage. Here is Ambria's story after her first year of lessons.

Ambria's Story:

"I'm not going to lie, my first year studying with Heidi was pretty intense. I was excited, nervous, and scared because I didn't know what was going to happen or what she might make me do. I had heard of the risks and the ways she pushed her other students to grow, so I wasn't sure what to expect. I like to have control over everything and when I don't, things feel overwhelming to me. My first couple of times singing on the studio Instagram were risks she helped me take. She encouraged me to sing in higher keys that I was not comfortable with yet but that actually helped me grow as a singer. At first, I kept thinking of the people I knew, that I didn't want to hear my 'not so perfect voice' or see my videos, but as I kept going, it got easier. Most people I knew hadn't even seen my videos, or so I thought. People started to compliment me on my songs, yet all I could think about was that they had seen my videos and how terrible they were. All these negative thoughts came flooding into my mind, so I couldn't even hear the good things people had to say. I would say to anyone who is too scared to try like I was/am, something to remember is that . . . YOU. ARE. NOT. ALONE. Almost everyone gets nervous and scared to put themselves out there. You just get used to it. The sad truth is that so many people just think about all the bad things people could say about them, so they don't even try. Then the world misses out on all they have to offer. There's only one you in the world, and you have to be it. Try your best not to let negative thoughts keep you from trying and achieving. It takes some time, and I'm definitely not all the way there yet, but compared to who I was at the beginning of the school year, I would say I've become a way more confident performer, and I hope that you all can push through fear and do whatever it is that you are called to do."

Fear is the enemy of greatness. Our incredibly complex bodies have fear programmed into them for a reason. If a bear approaches you, fear is a good thing. It is not the time to stand around rationalizing, it is time to flee for your life!! That kind of good fear is so necessary for our survival. It is the fear of something that is actually dangerous, whereas being afraid to be yourself, to sing in front of people, to share your art, or to dance is not the same kind of fear. That type of fear almost always comes from lie-based thought patterns. And the fun thing is, often when you really work at removing and replacing them, your entire life can change for the better. Take my student Paige, for example.

Paige's Story:

"When I first began studying with Heidi, everyday life was constantly interrupted by the fear I embodied. Something as simple as walking into school alone scared me. I was constantly in fear of people looking at me, what they would say about me, and what they would think about me. My own happiness was never a thought as I was consistently viewing my life from the opinions of others. Meeting new people was one of the scariest things to do. I never had an interest in going to a place where I didn't know every single person ahead of time. When Heidi started encouraging me to sing on a stage in public places, it started to affect my everyday life.

She did not allow me to say 'I can't' when I was frustrated playing an instrument, and that also began to translate to my everyday life. I will never say I can't do anything again because I know that I just have to work at it. Refusing to let negativity be a thing made my whole life positive. I'm now at the point in my life where meeting new people is my favourite thing to do. I enjoy having conversations with people I don't know and getting to hear their stories. All because of music."

As well as working on changing the beliefs that are usually the root systems causing the fear to manifest, I highly recommend actively working on your bravery muscle. I like to think of bravery as a muscle that gets stronger and stronger as you do more and more brave things. If you chip away at fear by cultivating a lifestyle of taking healthy risks, it's like chipping away at an ice wall with an axe. Eventually, after a lot of chops, you are going to break through it and that wall is going to come down. I challenge my fearful students to do fifty risks in a year or if that seems easy for them, a hundred! Notice that I said *healthy* risks. A healthy risk is something that's good for you that you are too scared of doing. The risks don't even have to be arts-related to flex your bravery muscle. If you want to do big, amazing, scary things someday, then it would be good to practice doing the little scary things first, right? If you've never posted any of your creations on your Instagram or social media, you will most likely be too afraid to do a radio or television interview. It's good to start with the small things when you start to take risks. The students who are more afraid tend to get through one hundred risks quicker because they are scared of so many more things. Common everyday risks for really shy people include raising your hand in class, giving a wrong answer in class, talking to people you don't know at school or at church, saying hello to people as you walk by, or talking to the cashier at Walmart. I had one student who was terrified of butter . . . You just never know what people are afraid of. I used to do a hundred risks a year to show students that I was on their side, and I faithfully did this for at least two years. The list of things that scared me kept getting smaller and smaller (which is the whole point if you hadn't figured that out yet). The list of things that scare me is now small. Parallel parking still gets me. I am not great at it, and sometimes it takes me six tries to get in between those two cars. I panic when there is a lineup of cars behind me honking and watching me try and fail on all the one-way streets in Winnipeg. Blech. Another one is loud sounds that draw everyone's attention to me in a public space. The bank that I go to has a large, old, black car horn mounted on a sign that says, 'honk if you had good service.' I look at it and think, "Heidi, what would your students think of you walking away from a risk?" I end up honking even if I got bad customer service. At Mongos Restaurant they have a loud gong that you hit with a mallet and the grills-men do a little 'hey hop' for you. I am mortified every time, but I know that I have to do it, so by sheer willpower, I hit that gong. Heyyyyyyy Hop!

    A useless fear that still sometimes gets me is dancing at an event. You dancers will probably find this next story very amusing, and I am also sure that after publishing this book, I will wake up with a vulnerability hangover, but I share it for the greater good. I grew up in a very religious environment where dancing was not allowed (like in *Footloose*). I was once told as a preteen that if I moved my hips when I walked, men would lust after me. Gulp. There's a whopper of a belief to remove! I wasn't allowed to go to school dances, take dance classes, or go to any parties in high school.

In university, however, dancing became a requirement when I had to learn to waltz for an opera scene I was cast in.

This was a mountain of a deal, and I may have cried (I actually mean buckets of tears). Not only did I have to waltz on stage in front of an audience, but I had to waltz going backwards, in a circle, in high heels, moving with a group of waltzers in an even larger circle, while singing opera in Italian!!

It was a fiasco, and I barely made it out alive. I had visions of myself pitching off the front of the stage with Winn (my waltz partner) and ruining the scene for the audience. For everyone else who had grown up dancing, it was no big deal. For me, it was a huge and painful trigger.

After surviving the waltzing, I decided I needed to gain some control over this situation and face this phobia so that the next time I had to dance, it would not be as traumatic. I started to take free Ukrainian dance classes (much crying) and tap classes, which I cried a little less about because I was in a class with seven-year-olds. After some years had passed, I began to gain confidence in my ability to move. However, social dancing at an event was another beast entirely because there was no one to tell me to 'shuffle ball change.' The number of evenings I spent shedding tears about social dancing is atrocious. It was also really disheartening because looking around the room, it always seemed like everyone else was having so much fun and that I was the only one missing out on it. I wanted so badly to join in and be good at it, but the fear I was carrying was paralyzing me.

Why do I share this right now with you? I want you to really understand how hard it was for me in the moment, so that when you are in a similar place, you will decide to be brave and push through whatever is holding you back, even if it's really painful. I remember one night about five years ago, I was determined to take another swing at dancing, and I bravely went to a public dance. My dear friend Lacey came to dance with me for the whole evening. A lot of other friends were there that night, but Lacey and I danced in the back corner to hide the fact that I was crying the whole time. I did not stop dancing the whole evening because I was determined to break fear's hold. That may sound so silly to those of you who aren't afraid of dancing. Often our irrational fears sound ridiculous to others but feel real to us. I am happy to say that today I am able to get on a dance floor without crying, and after one hour,

I am almost having a good time. One of my life's goals is to be able to dance unhindered in a public place.

The false beliefs embedded in fearful Heidi would be rooted in comparison. My thoughts back then went something like, 'I don't know how to move, what do I do next? I am not as good a dancer as the person next to me. Everyone can see I can't dance and am scared. Everyone is laughing at me. Everyone is staring at me. My butt looks fat. I am not dressed as nicely as everyone else. My clothes are ugly. My makeup is ugly. My hair is ugly. I don't belong. Everyone can see that I don't belong. I need to get out of here.' The thoughts would have spiralled even further down than that back then, and I probably would have let them because I had no concept that I could stop the negativity. Most of those thoughts weren't true, with the exception of not knowing how to dance, of course.

When you start stepping out and taking risks, these thoughts might pop up more often for the first while, but usually, the longer you practice taking risks, the quieter those voices get. Then you will be able to handle taking even bigger ones! Another concept I want to give you is that **risk equals opportunity**. That would be a good one to write down and think about.

There are lyrics from an Aubrey Logan song called "So Cute" that I love so much for this very reason. The song is about all the things she misses when she is on tour, like her cat. It has these two golden nuggets in here for you.

Lyrics to the end of the first verse:

> *"I miss my business bank account being in the black,*
> *But I don't miss sitting on the floor, twiddling my thumbs like that, never again."*

Lyrics to the end of the second verse:

> *"I miss blaming everybody else, including you,*
> *But I don't miss sitting on my butt, too afraid to lose.*[9]*"*

And I think it's exactly that. We only have one life. Sitting on our butts, too afraid to lose is not a good choice for us! This is why risks became such an important part of my studio, because they lead to the fantastical. So often now, students who used to dread singing for their parents post their singing online. The new students coming in who didn't sing for PTP come into this culture, and because of what was done before them, they actually make the transition quicker.

What I would say to you, if this chapter is where you are at, is to set a goal for yourself for taking healthy risks in the next six months, and just start! I would also tell someone you trust or a mentor what you are doing so that they can encourage you (and also so that you don't chicken out!). After a while, you might be surprised at the really neat opportunities that begin to come your way. If you go sing at an open mic, a big risk if you've never done it, there is a greater chance that someone will hear you and want to collaborate. Or you might meet someone who can give you the next steps you need to get where you are going. If you audition for a play, you might get the opportunity to perform with a cast of forty and gain a ton of useful stage experience. Letting someone see your original sculpture that isn't finished is a really vulnerable thing, but how else are you going to get feedback on it? I'll say it again, **risk equals opportunity,** so it's worth cultivating a culture of healthy risk in your life. You want to do this so that risking becomes part of your normal life. Some of the biggest risks I have taken have turned out to be the coolest things I have ever done.

MINDFUL MEDITATION:

"I face the new with confidence. I am abundance. I trust my inspiration. I am fully supported and have all that is required to release my expression. I see my vision with clarity. I am enough. I am centred in love."

CHAPTER SUMMARY:

- Fear is the enemy of greatness.
- Risk equals opportunity.
- Cultivate a lifestyle of taking healthy risks.

QUESTIONS TO PONDER:

1) What are some of the irrational things that I am afraid of? Why am I afraid of them?
2) Is fear holding me back in my craft? How?
3) What are some healthy risks that I can take right now?

NOTES:

_____
_____
_____
_____
_____
_____
_____
_____

CHAPTER 6
COMPARISON

"Originals are not always supposed to fit in, and we need to be ok with that."

Ray Hughes

Some of the negative thoughts you might hear in your head will have to do with the nasty beast called Comparison. Comparison is a major joy-killer if you let it sit upon the throne of your mind. It is a sure-fire way of fast-tracking you to the mopey place (see the upcoming chapter). What I am going to tell you next is something that I have literally absorbed into my skin, and it is one of the things that keeps me really steady as an artist and a person. I think of myself as a horse with blinders on, walking or running forward toward my goal. I just Googled blinders and found out they are actually called 'blinkers'—how funny. Well, those blinkers prevent a horse from being distracted or spooked by crowds on city streets, and in racing, they also help the horse stay focused on the finish line. I picture myself that way because I don't want to get side-railed by looking at how much better the singer to the left of me is, how far ahead of me they are, or how much more even their vibrato is than mine. I need to keep my eyes forward and on the unique race that I am running.

> *"I think the main thing I could tell anybody starting out is to not compare yourself to other people. Everyone else is on a different path than you, and I know it might seem like everyone else is on the same path but all those finish lines that you're thinking of in your head . . . everyone has their own finish line. Don't let others dim your light, and just keep being yourself and that is all you need."*
>
> *Ryan Nealon – Singer-Songwriter, Recording Artist*

No one's story is exactly like yours, so why would you even bother comparing yourself to them in the first place? Here's the concept: **the only person I can compare myself to is myself from last year.** Grab that. I mean really grab that. Am I better than I was last year? Yes. Good. Have I learned one thing this month? Yes. Good. If this is your attitude, you won't be crossing over into another racer's lane and wasting time in their race. If you picture a horse swinging into the other lanes sporadically, that takes away precious time and energy needed to get where they want to go and can often cause a stall. My student Maya, who has a stunningly beautiful singing voice and a ton of natural musical ability, experienced this growing up with a sister who was equally musical. It was easy for her to fix her eyes on her sister's voice and skill while at the same time remaining completely blind to how beautiful an instrument she had been given herself.

Maya's Story:

"I've often compared myself to my wildly talented, natural songbird of a sister. I admire her unique sound and have envied her for all the praise she gets from my parents (whose opinions I deeply care about), friends, and professional artists. I've sometimes thought to myself, 'why do I even try? I'm never going to be as good at songwriting and singing as she is, so I should just find another talent.' But the problem is, I love to sing. That's the key. I think the thing that helped me grow more confident in the sound of my voice was finding songs and genres that suited me, that I loved and related to, and that matched my range and style. I've since found that I love the sound of my voice."

Here is the truth: If I compare my journey to, say, that of my absolute favourite singer, I cannot. Even though she is only four years older than me, she has travelled the world, played to sold-out audiences in big venues, released four albums, and been the lead in multiple musicals on Broadway. If I compare my situation to hers, I will easily get pulled toward depression. Depression is an immobilizer. It causes your journey to halt to a standstill and gets your eyes focused inward instead of forward. After spending way too much time in that zone as a twenty-year-old, I now avoid comparison **at all costs**. This singer had a very different start than I did. She got to take dance classes, was exposed to jazz, soul, and musical theatre at a young age, and was given so many opportunities. If she had been raised with my isolated upbringing, her path would be different. Full stop. **We can't mourn our beginnings**. It doesn't matter where we started, what matters is what we have done with our life. If you are just learning how to dance at age thirty-seven, thank God you get to learn how to dance! If you are picking up a pen and paper to write spoken words at age fifty, go for it! We need to hold gratitude in our hearts daily for our own unique journeys rather than mourning the fact that we are not as far as we'd like or that someone else is ahead of us. News flash— **there will always be someone ahead of you.**

One of my students Kevin was a prime example of someone who was crippled by comparison. He had the attitude of 'I am never going to be as good as this other person, so why should I even bother practicing?' For his entire first year of lessons, he wallowed in that negative headspace.

Kevin's Story:

"When I first started taking music lessons, I was filled with unreal expectations and the belief that it should be easy to meet them. As I began to realize I wasn't going to arrive at the 'skilled musician station' without effort, time, and loads of practice, I began to grumble and complain. I figured I was entitled to have musical capabilities simply handed to me, and because of that mindset, the progress I managed to make during my first year was limited. I compared what little growth I had achieved to what I'd been expecting to become (a pop star at the top of the charts), and I saw nothing but disappointment. I constantly spoke awful words over myself and believed them. I said things like: 'I'll never get it, so why even try?' or 'I'm not getting anywhere, so maybe I'll quit lessons and learn on my own.' I wanted to give up because I thought I wasn't getting a big enough reward for the work I put in. As lessons went on, and with practice, Heidi and I righted the wrong pathways in my brain. Every time I said something degrading about myself, Heidi stopped me and told me to speak out the truth about the situation. I started saying things like: 'This is hard, but I'll get it soon,' and 'Man, look at how far I've come since last year!' When I look back on those days, I see how my musical growth began to increase exponentially. As I began to believe I could, I did. I still had to do the hard work I dreaded, but the results were finally noticeable. Instead of comparing myself to professionals with years of experience in the industry, I compared myself to who I was a year ago or even a month ago. I celebrated every jump forward, and I faced the difficult times head on. My focus wasn't on what I couldn't do, but on what I could do and would soon be able to do. Music became fun instead of being a chore. I still had to force myself to practice, but I did it happily, and I knew there might be a cool new skill or piece of knowledge right around the corner. This excitement of what could be next, and all the little moments along the way, spurred me on. Now I'm a confident singer who tries new techniques shamelessly (even if people might hear me crack or make a weird noise), and I'll happily sing in public when people ask me to. It's no longer about perfection. It's about blessing people with the gift I've been working on and communicating something. Instead of feeling like quitting due to the fact that I am not perfect, I have found that people can connect with me easier because I'm not perfect."

Kevin exploded musically the moment he learned mastery over his own mind. I entrusted him with the role of student teacher in my music studio. Kevin has written at least forty songs now, is an authentic communicator, and was also cast as the lead in his school's production of *Fiddler on the Roof*. He financed his music lessons by teaching for me, and he worked in a turkey barn for a year to pay for his schooling in the United States. Old Kevin would have said, "Nothing good is ever going to happen to me, so why dream?" New Kevin knows that nothing is impossible. Say that out loud over yourself. **"Nothing is impossible."**

> *"Individuality is more important than ever. I really encourage you not to pattern yourself after anybody.* **Being unique is the most magical gift you can have**. *Wait it out and continue to show up. Eventually the perfect vehicle for you is going to come up. Don't change to fit a system that's always changing anyways. The sooner that you can fall in love with who you are, and be proud of your differences, that is the key to being successful."*
>
> ***Shoshana Bean*** [10]

Carol, a former student, never told me about her inner struggle with comparison during our years together. It never interfered with her growth in lessons, so when she sent me her writing for this book, I was so surprised to read that she had wrestled with it! Here are her thoughts and how she talks herself through it.

Carol's Story:

"One of the biggest obstacles in my music journey in the past would probably be comparison. I still struggle with it at times, if I'm honest. I get caught up in the mindset of, 'there's always going to be someone better than me, so why bother?' That's true—there are always people who are going to be more talented than you. That's why this mindset is so harmful. It twists you into believing what you have to offer isn't important, beautiful, or powerful.

"I would usually slip into this belief when I saw a specific person performing who was really gifted in something I'd like to be good at. This happened the most when I compared myself to other vocalists I knew personally. It's really easy for me to see a friend perform, notice something specific, such as how well-controlled their voice is, and wish I could sing like that. What I'm not taking into consideration, though, is that there are most likely areas that I might be more talented in. **It's easy to focus on what you're not instead of realizing all that you are.**

"I've learned to recognize that someone's seemingly perfect performance involves a lot of unseen hard work and practice. I can't be expecting my three weeks of practice to look as good as someone else's three years.

"Also, if I'm rehearsing my craft with the goal of being exactly like another musician or vocalist, I'm going to come up short. Instead of wishing I was as good as someone else, I often need to remind myself to look back on my own journey. I need to be reminded of how far I've come. Yes, I've accomplished many things on my own music journey that are worth celebrating. That's the exciting thing—there's always more to learn. Everyone's artistic journey is unique. They are all beautiful and can be just as impactful as another."

Haven Peckover – Canadian Visual Artist

"Comparison is definitely a big thing. I think especially because I grew up as technology was advancing, and it became harder to escape looking at reference images of master painters or even people around me who were doing better work than I was. That always kind of comes up, and I think that is just the way things work now when you are really dedicated to a craft. That little sneaky snake comes in and tells you that you aren't doing enough, you aren't good enough, and that you aren't going to get there, so it's something you have to push down a lot. I don't struggle with it as much anymore, just being a little more mature and less focused on other people when it comes to something that I love and know that I was born to do.

"I think there is a pretty big difference between comparison and taking inspiration from people. I think a lot of people confuse the two. You can look at reference images, and you can study old masters and try to copy the painting exactly and try to figure out how they did all these things, but they are two completely different things. You can't compare yourself to somebody that doesn't have the tools that you have now. But you can try to recreate what they did, and then work from that and create your own style from that. It's so hard with the internet now too. There are so many new images, so many new artists popping up that you feel like you need to be where they are in terms of numbers, but if you're taking inspiration from their work, how they create, the mediums they use, and the process that they go through, I think that definitely helps you as a creative person. **Nobody is totally original.** We are all taking bits and pieces of things that have happened in history, so it's something you can't really avoid. Numbers don't matter as long as you're gaining experience and people are reaching out to you for your experience."

> *"Authenticity. Be Authentic. Whatever makes your voice your voice, your sound your sound, lean into it. Devour it. It's something that makes you you, that no one else has."*
>
> *Therese Curatolo – Singer-Songwriter, Performer, Recording Artist*

Here is a quick disclaimer though before we wrap up. Comparison, when you are grounded in your own identity and can embrace your imperfections, can be such a valuable teacher. If I look at someone ahead of me skill-wise, I can look at my work and see the very things that I need to improve and grow in. A lot of my learning is done by listening and watching those who are ahead of me skill-wise and career-wise. It would be the same thing for a dancer. It's the super-skilled, mind-blowing, jaw-dropping dancers that can inspire you to work harder and better yourself. Again, that type of thinking isn't for the beginners. You must have your identity settled to be able to use comparison as your ally. Only you will know if you are still vulnerable in this area. If you are, I highly recommend the 'blinder' approach until you are really comfortable being in your own skin and have eliminated a good chunk of your negative beliefs. Once you have removed comparison as a hindrance, then it can become invaluable when used carefully and intentionally. Also, in listening, watching, and studying other people's work, some of the flavour of what they carry can seep into yours and elevate your game.

MINDFUL MEDITATION:

"I embrace my unique expression. I step out of the box and into the new. I am safe and accept who I am. I am true to who I am and move forward with ease. While I appreciate others, I am focused on my vision. I see clearly."

CHAPTER SUMMARY:

- The only person I can compare myself to is myself from last year.
- Where you begin doesn't matter; make the most of your life.
- Realize all that you are instead of focusing on what you're not.

QUESTIONS TO PONDER:

1) Who do I compare myself with?
2) What is the result of comparison in my life?
3) Does comparison cripple me or catapult me forward? If it cripples me, what is the false belief I am holding on to in this area? What is a true statement I can begin to put there instead?

NOTES:

_____
_____
_____
_____
_____
_____
_____
_____

CHAPTER 7
REJECTION

Rejection in the artistic industry is such a given. It is impossible to be any kind of artist and not experience the sting of rejection. If you have never experienced rejection, you are either hidden away so that no one sees your work, or you are a magical unicorn. Rejection in the arts is everywhere; your audition goes poorly, your novel isn't accepted for publishing, you don't get any bookings for your spoken word, or your YouTube video only has ten views, nine of which are from your mother. If you are not careful, rejection can create negative beliefs that will permeate your defences and immobilize you. You must be the gatekeeper here. After the initial sorrow of being rejected, if you wallow in it too long, thoughts like, 'I'll never make it,' 'No one likes me, they hate me,' 'Everyone hates my art,' 'Things are hopeless,' 'I guess I am not talented,' etc. will slide their way into your mind. If you don't guard against that, what happens is a standstill effect, sometimes a walking-away from your craft if it was a bad rejection.

A couple of years ago, I filmed a fishing music video with my dad for his seventieth birthday. After the view count stopped rising, I started sending it places in hopes that someone would come alongside me and help me promote it. My first responses were rejections. I received nine rejections in a row, and one of them was what I would call an 'ugly rejection.' This is what this man wrote: "Hi Heidi. Cute song, pretty voice, not our style." Maybe that doesn't sound so bad to you, but cute and pretty are not my favourite words, especially when used to describe myself or my voice. Funny thing was, it was this tiny radio station from my hometown that should have supported me. BUT the tenth news station I sent it to absolutely loved it and sent a news vehicle two hours north to interview my dad and I. The feature was broadcast nationwide across Canada, which was so cool! If I had given up after the nine rejections, I would have never had the excitement of seeing my dad and I on television together (the story is not about me though—wait for it). The point of this story is people will reject your art, your voice, your creations . . . and **it's okay**. It's okay to be rejected. It doesn't mean your art isn't worthwhile. It doesn't mean you don't have something to say. It doesn't mean that you are 'doomed to fail.' It just means that maybe you weren't their cup of tea. That doesn't mean you won't be someone else's. Keep putting your art out there. If people give you helpful feedback, take it and grow from it. If they call your art 'cute' and your voice 'pretty,' then move on. Keep knocking on doors. Keep knocking. Knock knock knock. Keep growing while you keep knocking. Never stop growing. Grow while you knock.

Rejection isn't always fair either. It really depends on the spirit of the person giving it to you. If they are emotionally unhealthy themselves, often the rejection can be much more mean-spirited. My student Janelle experienced this firsthand growing up in competitive dance. It breaks my heart to think about all she was put through unfairly.

Janelle's Story:

"I was three when I started dancing at a studio in Winnipeg, Manitoba. I had stage fright and refused to perform in any capacity for two years. Then I turned six and decided it was time for me to perform with the rest of the group. Because of my height and size, I was placed in the back and in the middle. This never bothered me because I was always the centre of the dance, which was fun to me; to be at the centre of the number meant the centre of attention. Every performance made me fall further in love with the art, and I participated in every single style I could, taking up to seven classes each week. It wasn't until I started dancing competitively that everything changed.

"I knew I was taller than everyone, and I grew up taking pride in that and bragging about being the tallest in school or in dance class, but I never realized how much my weight would later come into play. I believe in being kind to anyone and everyone and not colouring that vision until proven otherwise, but in my later years of dance, those around me did not share the same view. I started struggling with body image in my elementary school years, but it didn't start in dance until I was in competitive classes. I was struggling by looking around the room at every girl who was ten sizes smaller than me, and it started to affect my mental health.

"In a ballet class about five years before I left the studio, we were doing floor exercises, and I wasn't doing the step as well as the other girls. The teacher was walking around the room and approached me. I continued to do the actions until she asked everyone to stop and instructed us on the next one. I didn't think anything of it (because she was looking at all the other dancers as well) until she pulled me aside after class. Her words were extremely damaging: 'You just aren't built to be a ballerina.'

"The last year I was in dance, I was invited into the top level of competitive jazz with all the girls who travelled the world for competitions and even some world champions. They were all 120 pounds and five foot two, the same hair colour, with little variation in their looks. I, obviously, did not look the same and that was hard for me to understand. One class in particular pushed me over the edge. The teacher was always very strict and intense, so I made myself work as hard as I possibly could. I have always been a person who sweats a lot when doing activity, and she took notice of that and said, 'You really do sweat a lot, Janelle, you should work on that,' and those words have never left me. Sweating is now associated with negativity and being too big to do anything. That is never how it should be viewed. I worked hard every day in those classes, and because of something I couldn't control, I felt that I had to drop out.

"My experiences are my own, and not everyone is going to feel the same way or be told the same things. In dance classes, those thoughts and feelings transferred into my everyday life, and I started becoming even more insecure going anywhere because I thought I was too big and everyone would stare at me. My mental health revolved around how I appeared to others rather than how I felt about myself and in my own body. I was never able to go to class without makeup or without wearing a sweater so no one would see my body. I was so conditioned to believe that I wasn't beautiful without it. In my experiences with dance classes, I felt excluded and ignored because of my size. My mental health became so bad that at the end of my thirteenth year of dance, I quit, and I found another passion in musical theatre. Now almost three years later, my mental health has improved dramatically. I feel beautiful in my own skin for the first time and have found things that make me feel good like singing and playing the piano. For so many years, I thought I was not worthy of love, when in reality, I had been trained to believe that I didn't fit in. Finding out that who I am is beautiful in and of itself was the turning point for my recovery to who I am today: talented, beautiful, and so, so worthy!"

Right? I love that ending. I love seeing Janelle's posts on social media and watching the amazingly confident woman she is becoming. Another student of mine who experienced painful rejection from her peers at a young age was held hostage by it in her musical journey.

She was so afraid of being rejected again that she refused to sing online or anywhere her friends might one day see it and disapprove.

Linnea's Story:

"Growing up, I was not very popular, and I would get made fun of by my peers. I never used to let it get to me as much as I did as I got older, but when I got to junior high and high school, I started wanting people to like me, and I would seek their approval. This had a big impact on my music because every time I wrote something or performed in front of others, I wanted them to like what I was showing them. I needed others to tell me that they approved of what I was doing and that they were impressed. I lived to hear people tell me that they liked what I was doing.

"I think this need for acceptance stemmed from low self-esteem. I would let fear of rejection control my decisions and how my life played out. I would not share my music online or post videos of what I worked hard on. Having my music posted where everyone could see it and have negative opinions on it was too scary. The thought of opening up to my peers and people I saw in my day-to-day world by giving them access to such a hidden and private part of my life made me afraid. What if I wasn't good enough? What if they thought I was bad? What if they talked about me and I got made fun of again? I didn't want to go back to that part of my life. I was past that. People were starting to like me, and I didn't want to jeopardize that.

"I now realize that that way of thinking was only making things harder for me. As of today, I have not overcome that fear completely, but I have come more to terms with the fact that no matter what I do, there is going to be someone who will have something negative to say about it. My goal for the future is to be able to not let others stop me from doing what I love to do and to do it proudly."

Remember that iceberg analogy? If your worth is in the unseen parts of you, when the storm of rejection comes, or people's nasty words hit you, your goal is to remain firm and unshakeable. You want to be like a big oak tree with its root system going down deep into the ground. It can't be knocked over by a prairie windstorm easily. A tree with shallow roots doesn't stand a chance.

MINDFUL MEDITATION:

"I love who I am. I am divinely connected and have endless sources: I am true to who I am and allow myself to be real. I embrace the process of my journey. I breathe deeply and remain centred in joy. Peace is mine."

CHAPTER SUMMARY:

- Rejection happens, but you are not a reject.
- Guard your thoughts when you get rejected.
- Don't stop knocking, and don't stop growing.

QUESTIONS TO PONDER:

1) How do people's critiques of my art affect me?
2) How do I handle rejection? Do I see it as a personal rejection of self?
3) Am I carrying any battle wounds from past rejections that are influencing me negatively today?

NOTES:

CHAPTER 8

FEEDBACK AND WHO SHOULD GIVE IT TO YOU?

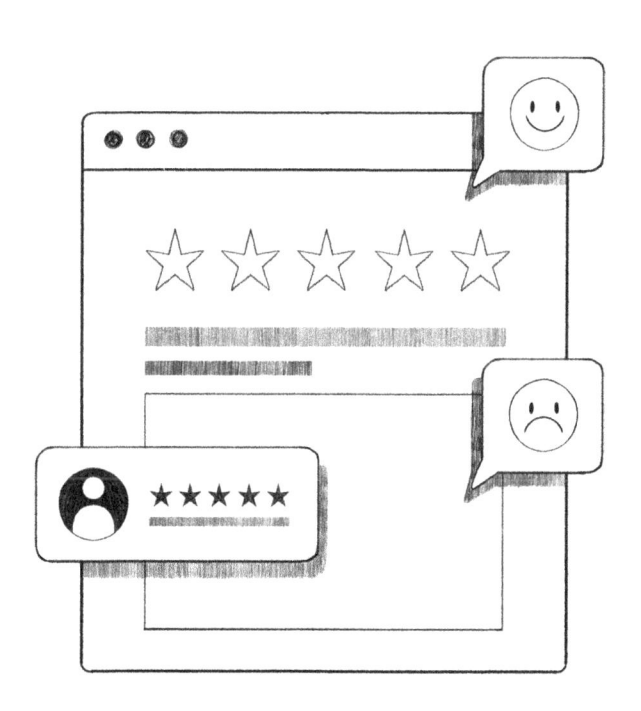

We chant things like 'sticks and stones may break my bones, but words will never hurt me,' but in actuality, we all know words can hurt. Rejection hurts. Criticism hurts. But . . . feedback is essential for growth. So, who do you listen to? Whose words do you trust and let through the shield that you develop around your heart when there is so much feedback coming your way? Something that helps me keep grounded is to allow a small group of people, whose words really matter to me, to speak into my life and give me honest reviews about my art. I don't give the key to my artist heart to just anyone. If I do, it will get broken so easily. I have about four or five people who, when they say, "Heidi, you can do better than that," or "Heidi, that was great," I take seriously because they know me, what I am capable of, and what I have done in the past. A couple of these people are musicians in my field who are ahead of me and that I have relationships with. I also know these people won't compliment me falsely. An ex-boyfriend of mine, on a date, told me straight up that my YouTube videos were ugly **on the day** that I had just released one I was quite proud of. While his timing and the language he used were poor choices, once I cooled down, I realized he was right and began learning about backdrops and lighting. This improved my visuals tremendously, and I have him to thank for that growth. His feedback really caused me to level up. At the time, I wanted to punch him in the face, but in this moment, I have nothing but gratitude. The other people whose opinions should matter are those of your coaches, mentors, directors, and people you are hired by or are learning from.

Mike Bickle told this story: "*I heard the story of a concert pianist in the last century who longed to play in the great concert hall in Vienna. When he finished his first concert before thousands, the people gave him a long standing ovation. Afterwards, he was asked, 'Was it the greatest moment in your life to receive this long applause?' The concert pianist replied, 'No! I liked it, but it was not the most important thing to me.' He said, 'When the people all sat down, an elderly man who sat in the top corner of the balcony simply nodded his head at me. That was the greatest moment of my life because he is the master who taught me for thirty years. One nod from him was worth much more than the long applause from the masses.'*"

The words of a stranger aren't always true and good for you. When I sing in public, so many people will come up and say that I did a good job and that I have a great voice. But there are also times when I've sung where the audience has been checking their phones or some annoying person in the club has been talking and laughing loudly over my song. (**cough** holding in the name of a friend who did this). There was even a time I came offstage and a stranger came right up to me to tell me all the things I should have done differently, which I think is the worst thing to do to a performer that you don't know and don't have a relationship with. I have done this only one time in my life to a young performer. If you are that performer and you are reading this, I am so sorry! I have not forgotten you, and I have carried that mistake with me. Never do this to anyone. Your motives for giving feedback to the artist might be to help, but if you don't have a relationship with them, or they are not asking you in a natural way, then, as my friend Julie Meyer would say, "Put a cork in it!"

The words of a stranger can sometimes be beneficial, but it will be for you to judge and weigh carefully what they are saying and decide if there is truth in it for you to let in and grow from. For you performers, if your performance wasn't well received, or you are unsure of how it went, I highly recommend filming yourself so you can watch it back later, analyze how it went, and give yourself notes on how you can improve.

It's easy when we have a phone-checking audience to believe the lies that we are awful, nobody likes us, and we will never get anywhere, but how about we just don't go down that rabbit hole at all? You might have been singing jazz in a region where people love country music. It's okay. Keep your head in check.

If the audience wasn't engaged with me, was it because I wasn't authentic, present, or communicating my lyrics? Was it the wrong style for the venue? Was my skill sloppy that evening? The key to knowing this is sometimes in watching your playback. If you never watch your performances, you might never know the answer, and your improvement might be slower because you will be relying solely on how you 'think it went,' which isn't reliable.

If you are a performer/singer/actor/dancer and have never done this, let me prepare you now. The first time you do it, you might feel like quitting entirely. You might also have some pretty big emotional moments. Don't walk away. Watching yourself is a little easier for dancers and much harder for young singers and actors starting out who have not heard their own voices recorded back. I will take a moment to help the speaking creatives who are reading this book. If you don't know this, you normally hear your own voice in a way that no one else does, it's super strange. We hear our own throat's sound waves sent out into the air, but we also hear our sound being carried up to our ears by our jawbone. If you plug your ears tight and talk, you will be able to hear your jawbone vibration. Take a second to do this and listen to how muddled the jawbone vibration is and how it is not as clear as the sound that's in the air. Our incredible ears actually take those two different sounds and interpret them as one sound: our voice. The voice you hear in your head is actually more like a double of you because of those bone vibrations and no one but you can hear that. When you listen back to yourself recorded for the first time, you are hearing what the rest of the world hears, which can be quite startling and off-putting at first, especially if it's been recorded by a low-quality phone microphone. The first time my students listen back to themselves singing, they often make huge fusses and exclaim things like: "That sounds weird," "That doesn't sound as good," or "That sounds so bad." There are sometimes tears, and in that moment, they feel the weight of discouragement pretty heavily. If you have never done this, the homework I would give you is to record your voice on a device and listen back to it over and over again until there is no emotional response from your stomach. Once you achieve the feeling of calm acceptance that, 'This is my voice, and I can deal with it,' you will have conquered a small mountain! Congratulations! By reviewing your performances, you will be able to pick out the things you don't like and improve them much faster, which gives you much **more control** over your result. Sometimes I have recorded an upcoming performance eight times to eliminate all the things I disliked about my first try at it. The practice of reviewing your performances is especially helpful when there is no one you trust to give you feedback in that moment. Here is my student Jesse telling you all about her first time watching her playbacks.

Jesse's Story:

"Watching yourself perform or sing for the very first time is probably one of the most cringy moments. I remember saying to myself, 'Oh my gawd! Why do I sound like that?' From hearing yourself in the shower through the echoes in the bathroom, to listening to yourself on a recording, wow, you sound different. But the reason I sounded so horrible to myself was because I wanted perfection from my voice. Even when I felt like I sang something perfectly, I always found little parts where I flinched or made a face because I didn't like the sound. Much the same with my voice in general, when I hear myself speak on a recording, I think I sound annoying or I am hard on myself for no reason other than not seeing perfection. No matter where you are on your journey, you are always going to find imperfection. And you are going to struggle hard if you demand perfection out of yourself all of the time.

"At the age of ten, let me tell you, no one should be upset if their voice does not sound Beyoncé-like. It's great to have goals and achieve them one day, but that is achieved by taking little steps forward and practicing. It takes the realization that no one is perfect, and that the only way to get to be the best you can is just to try your hardest and learn to live with the after-effects. Mistakes are how you develop, and they show that you are a real human being. They are why people will feel connected with you, when you can perform and be comfortable with yourself no matter what goes down on stage (because, I mean really, our Instagram bloopers are the best part). Learning to laugh at myself is something I have gotten really good at, and it has taken me a long way from being embarrassed with my own voice to appreciating it and being excited about how far I can go with it. A journey is a beautiful thing, and you need to love it instead of just focusing on the end. Growing is something you will never stop doing, and even when you have reached a point where you have become something you want, you can still keep growing. Your art is something you should be thankful for, treat it with respect, and don't be afraid to embrace your uniqueness. Authenticity is a word that I have learned over the past few years, and it has taught me that no matter how skilled you are in your voice, if you have no originality or real meaningful feeling behind it, the sound has no value to it. Learn from the best, but do not try to be them. Love where you are at on your journey, because the road you are on can only go further."

Well put, Jesse. I couldn't have said it any better myself.

MINDFUL MEDITATION:

"I embrace truth. I receive input from those of my choosing. I choose to learn from experience. I am not identified by my process. I manifest divine in me. I choose growth. I am safe."

CHAPTER SUMMARY:

- Feedback is essential to growth. Don't be afraid of it, even if it's negative.
- Have a small amount of people you trust to give you feedback.
- Weigh carefully the feedback that you get from strangers.
- If applicable to your art form, begin to watch your performances back so you can give yourself notes.

QUESTIONS TO PONDER:

1) Who are the people I trust to give me constructive criticism? Do I need more?

2) Do I ever send my art to people who are further along than me for feedback?

3) Am I comfortable watching myself and giving myself constructive feedback?

NOTES:

CHAPTER 9
PERFECTIONISM

"Performances should never be perfect. There should always be risk involved. Otherwise, why would I spend eighty dollars on a ticket to see you perform, when I could spend that eighty dollars on a nice bottle of scotch and stay home and listen to the recording?"

John McMillan – Composer for Film, Television, and Video Games

I believe there is a fine line when it comes to perfectionism. When a perfectionist comes into my studio, it isn't always an apparent obstacle right away. Perfectionists are often great learners. What I love about teaching them is that they usually have really fantastic practicing habits, so whatever I assign them is usually done to task within the deadline I give them. However, there is an avalanche-sized downside to being a rigid perfectionist. I often see them hide away, cry after one mistake, break down, and burn out more than any of my other students. The lie that a rigid perfectionist believes is that 'if it's not perfect, it's not good enough.' There's a false belief that will really throw you if you let it.

I really don't know if it's possible to be a rigid perfectionist and survive in the industry. From my experience teaching, I see perfectionists stalling on their projects because they are afraid to release them to the world and have there be a mistake in it. You may look at a professional in your field and tell me their work is perfect, but I bet you they would acknowledge imperfection in their work that you are just not perceiving at your skill level. In my first hired composition "Wake up Yesterday," I thought I was killing it with my mad genius, but that was because I hadn't developed the ears to hear the fairly major flaws that were there. When I listen back now, I am horrified at my recording job. A beginner would listen to my track and exclaim, "Heidi, that's incredible!" A professional, however, would say, "Okay, that's a good start," and proceed to give me sixty notes on what to do better. Gulp. Thanks. All this is to say you will never be perfect. As Andrew Huang, a successful producer, artist, YouTuber, and influencer, says, "There is no perfect, there is only finished." Ray Hughes, author of over a thousand songs, said to me, "It's not ever going to be finished, but you have to know when to turn it loose."

Sometimes when people hear me say perfectionism isn't good, they think I am advocating for sloppiness, or anything less than one's best. Here is the difference: perfectionism will say that your best wasn't good enough and you should have done better. There, my friends, is the line and the lie. The truth is your best **is** good enough. Your best is also something that changes and evolves the more you continue to grow. My best two years ago is WAY different than my best now. There is also no way back then that I could have been anything more than I was. My first music video was called "Yes Cry," and it was a song I wrote about my personal faith. The problem was neither the director nor I had any experience filming music videos. The morning of the shoot, I chose not to stop for breakfast as I was late because of a snowstorm. My makeup was rushed, then I panicked and picked my outfit in a flurry, and I arrived late to the shoot. By the third hour of filming with no food or water, I was drained and unable to give a good performance. Why would I be so unprepared, you ask? Well, because I had no idea what I was doing! Question—How do you learn to get good at shooting a music video? Answer—by shooting one! Failure really is your best instructor. For my next music video, we shot it over two days, food was at the shoot, and my appearance was meticulously planned. I fixed all the problems from the first shoot but made fifteen brand-new mistakes in that one. No matter what stage of success you are at, beginner, intermediate, or professional, the concept is the same. Failure teaches you how to do it better the next time. Failure is actually your best teacher; it is not to be feared.

When I first heard one of Naomi's original songs, I fell in love with her writing style. I couldn't understand why, with such great songs, she was so very terrified to sing for me. I chalked that up to it being her first couple lessons and didn't realize until later that I was one of the first people she had shared her original music with—when she had already written about forty songs! Even her own family wasn't privy to hearing these. I'll let her explain why.

Naomi's Story:

"For a long time, I held myself hostage in my mind. I let fear stop me from doing the things I was passionate about. I had this toxic mentality that I was not talented enough. I convinced myself that I would share my music with people when I got better. But that was the thing, no matter what level I reached, no matter how much I practiced, it was never good enough because I didn't believe I was good enough. I wanted my music to be perfect, and I hated myself because no matter how hard I strived to achieve this perfection, it was out of my reach. I slowly lost my passion for creating music because of the pressure I put on myself, but you see, music is not meant to punish us. Creating is meant to express the innermost parts of ourselves in our own unique way. I let fear run my life for a very long time until eventually, I realized that it does not matter if it is not perfect because it never will be. My music is an expression of myself, and I am a progressing person, not a perfect person. Therefore, sharing my music will be a progression of my talent, a documented timeline to look back on and see where I was and how far I've come. The question you have to ask yourself is, who are you creating for? Do you want your creativity to be held captive within your bedroom walls? Or do you want to use it to express your soul and help people who relate and who will feel comfort in your creation? The choice is yours truly. But from someone who has been in that place before, let go of that fear and anxiety, and don't let it control you or hold you back. Silence the negative thoughts that whisper lies into your mind. Start speaking life into yourself; speak affirmations as a reminder that you are talented and worthy. Nothing good ever came from fear, so step out of yours and into a place of endless possibilities."

Aleta started studying with me virtually, wanting to learn how to play piano with a band. Honestly, the way to get good at playing in a band is by learning how to improvise (i.e., learning to create spontaneously in the moment). Aleta was someone who loved perfection and planning everything out and would get so scared to improvise before lessons with me that she would actually get nauseous. She wrote for the book in the middle of that struggle, and then asked if she could add a part two a year later. Here they are . . .

Aleta's Story:

Year One:
"I don't like trying things that I don't know how to do ahead of time. I try to impress people in everything I do. I think that if I mess up or if it doesn't turn out right, people will judge me, and I want everybody to think that I'm an amazing person. I don't want anyone to see me as anything less than perfect. Something related to that is improvising. I don't like improvising. I love knowing exactly what I'm supposed to do, and

I love it when there is a wrong way and a right way. Improvising is a lot more experimenting and is more just play what you feel. I've never done anything like it. Once I actually get to improvising, it isn't that bad. I keep my mind blank, and I just don't think about it. I get through it, but after I'm done, I realize that I was very tense. I was fearful the whole time, and sometimes I even catch myself holding my breath. I even feel sick sometimes before a lesson because I know Heidi will ask me to improvise."

Year Two:
"I have gained so much peace and confidence in the last eight months. I still have fear, but I have really grown. Improvising is not as big of a deal now. I give myself a five-to-ten-second pep-talk, take a deep breath, and just do it. When I start, I even have fun doing it. The whole situation with improvising also made it so much easier to start singing in front of Heidi. When I'm learning something new, I'm much calmer too. It goes beyond music. I am now an overall more confident person. Everything I have learned in the mental area of music has helped me for life in general."

Victoria Patterson – Dancer, Dance Instructor, Administrator

"In younger dancers, perfectionism comes up really early. I see some of the five- and six-year-olds I work with getting mad at themselves because they are not getting a step properly, and that keeps building in them all the way up through the levels. In my classes, I try to use language like 'as best as you can' because in their minds 'getting it right' means perfection. When you're dancing in a studio, it's competitive, and by being competitive, there is pressure added to the mix. Pressure to be perfect, pressure not to let down your teammates or your parents or to do well in competitions. Studying post-secondary dance is somewhat competitive because you are fighting for your grade, but you are really there to explore your artistry and to grow as a human. When you're in a dance studio, you're there to compete, and you have people counting on you. The repetition of 'do this again and again until it looks right' is how dancer's minds are trained as well as their bodies, which can often breed an unhealthy level of perfectionism. In my experience teaching dancers, I see them thinking thoughts like, 'I made a mistake, I'm going to get in trouble,' 'I did this wrong, I'm not going to get a good mark,' and 'I went into the wrong line and messed it up for my group, and we aren't going to win because of me.' Young dancers are also often trying to impress their teachers, parents, teammates, or the judges. The competitive side is one of the big reasons, I believe, why that perfectionism mentality comes in.

"Body image is a big part of the world of dance as well. Dancers often feel like they need a certain look, body type, or a certain physical facility. There is a checklist of what they think they need to be. They need to be thin, flexible, able to kick up to their face, able to pull their leg behind their head, etc., etc. That checklist is so large in dance that not having all the boxes checked off often means mental health suffers with the belief that they are not enough or are inadequate. It's very unrealistic to have all those things checked off for one person. The perfect body, the perfect hair and makeup that you can do yourself, the flexibility, the timing, being good in multiple disciplines is a big one—ballet, tap, and jazz—and now the 'triple threat' is here too: can you be a dancer that sings and acts? It's a lot of pressure.

"There were some professional ballet institutions when I was in school less than five years ago that still had weekly weigh-ins. A male dancer I knew really well, who was in a Canadian university studying dance, had a teacher tell him at Christmastime, 'When you go home for Christmas and you get hungry, make sure you just have some tea instead.'"

Emily Solstice Tait – Dancer

"I overcome pressure in the industry by changing my focus; I focus on the collaborative nature of working with music, choreography, space, and dancing with others or relating to an audience. I make everything I do, even a solo, a collaboration or duet. This removes the focus on me and the pressure of perfection. I also build in structure to help keep me calm. If I am worried about not being prepared, I arrive an hour ahead to review everything and be ready. Putting in the time and work by building a schedule always relieves pressure because then you know you are thoughtfully arising to the challenge.

"I notice in dance culture that you have to be careful to not be a rule follower so much that you lose confidence in your own abilities. Dance can have such a strict culture that it takes away from one's confidence as an individual. The constant checking-in and protocols in that environment can be infantilizing and have a serious effect on mental health."

Ray Hughes – Master Level Creative

"We have to realize that as creatives, we are extremely valuable before and after the process, no matter what comes out of it, if we can break that curse of performance off of it. Poetry isn't supposed to sound like it is written, it's supposed to sound like something that fell out of your heart and mind and made your life make sense. Give yourself to your skill. Learn your craft, but don't struggle with the craft so much that you miss the beauty and the process."

Marietta Schultz – Watercolour Artist, Painter

"Find out what you love to paint. Is it landscapes? Flowers? People? What are your most favourite colours to paint with? Do you like contrast? If you enjoy what you are painting and enjoy the colours you are using, your entire process will be so much richer and enjoyable."

My students hear this from me a lot: How do you learn to write a song? By writing one! How do you learn to paint? By painting! Sometimes leaping into the deep end of the pool is how you learn to swim. Again, the unknown is a risk, so your risk muscles need to be ready, and rigid perfectionism really doesn't have a place. You will learn from each project, and then better yourself. Be okay with your absolute best now, and then just make sure to keep growing. Your best will grow and evolve the more projects you do.

MINDFUL MEDITATION:

"I am enough. What I am producing is enough. I have all that is required to finish what I have started. I am free to be who I am right at this moment and accept who I am in my journey. My artistic expression is enough in this moment as I move through life, progressing in my art. I express my best, and it is enough. I am loved."

CHAPTER SUMMARY:

- Rigid perfectionism is not an asset.
- Letting go of perfectionism doesn't mean you are sloppy.
- Your best is enough.
- Failure is a good teacher and not to be feared.
- Enjoying what you are doing is essential.

QUESTIONS TO PONDER:

1) What do I believe about myself when I make mistakes?
2) What is my emotional reaction when my work isn't perfect?
3) Can I love myself through my growing and learning?

NOTES:

CHAPTER 10
DISPLAYING PROCESS AND GETTING OVER EMBARRASSMENT

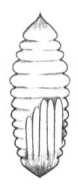

DON'T RUSH YOUR GROWTH IT'S A NATURAL PROCESS

I believe displaying process to be an essential part of defeating perfectionism. I have seen students frozen in fear learn to display process and come out of their cocoon like a butterfly. Displaying process allows you to stretch your authenticity muscle. There is a false belief there as well, which sounds like, 'I can't let anyone see anything that isn't perfect,' or 'I'll put out a song once I am sure that I'll never have another voice crack,' or 'I'll audition once I lose ten more pounds.' Sound familiar? This was the very thing that kept my musical life in chains during university. If I was back there now, I would force myself to practice in those horrid practice rooms, or I would bring a stereo and play rock music loudly in the room while I did my duck honk warmups.

Voice cracking on an operatic high note is still one of the most embarrassing things. I don't hear opera singers cracking on high notes very often, and in my small time spent in that community, there was not a ton of process or authenticity because of its formality (don't put the book down because you are an opera singer and are now offended. Keep reading.). In fact, back then, if I heard another singer crack or break on a high note, I would have thought to myself, 'They don't have their high notes sorted out. Who do they think they are trying for that song? Don't they know it's beyond their ability right now? They don't have what it takes.' When in reality, my high notes weren't perfect either, it was just that no one got to hear my cracks. This attitude that I used to carry myself at that time was toxic for others to be around and toxic for even myself. With Pass the Performance (see the introduction), I wanted to create a safe place online for all my students to sing—the advanced and the most beginner of beginners. There was a moment, though, if I am being honest with you, where I wondered if having my beginners participate in this very public project was going to hurt my reputation as a vocal coach. For a second, I made the mistake of making it about myself. I decided less than five minutes later that it was not going to be about my reputation, it was going to be about creating a safe space for my students to perform and support each other as a community. Five hundred days later, whenever a new singer joins us, right away the community welcomes them and cheers them on. I love it.

A lot of times people don't want to display themselves or their artwork because they are afraid of being embarrassed. I get that. In the ten years I have spent teaching teenagers and young adults, I often find they want to blend in with the grey walls and go unnoticed. Embarrassment is seen as the 'worst thing ever' and fear of it keeps the students from singing in their schools, auditioning for musicals, etc.

Something I do intentionally is leave my more cringy projects up online so my students can see that being a creative is a process. In that light, let's take a break from all our intense talk for me to share a funny embarrassment story with you. In summer of 2019, I was one of thirteen people invited to go to a creative conference in Santa Maria, California, and a sponsor decided to pay my way there and back (thank you!). While I was there, I was going to be working with talented people in the music industry, and I would be getting poured into instead of me pouring into others. Très exciting! Well. Well. Well. I get a text from the organizer of the event, also an established recording artist herself, about a week before this conference, saying, "Heidi, I just found this YouTube video of you with short blonde hair!" My insides immediately flip-flopped. "Which one?" I asked, praying to the Lord above that it was one of my better ones and not my very first split-screen video, which is one of the worst and most embarrassing things I have on the internet. (You are probably searching for it now on YouTube, aren't you? *Sigh.* Go ahead. I for sure can't take it down now after all my preaching on showing process.) Unfortunately, it was the exact video I feared that she had found. What was worse was she was so excited about it that she sent it to every staff member and musician who was coming to teach at the creative conference so they could get a sense of who I was. What. A. Moment. I remember sitting there and soaking that in, thinking to myself, *Wow, that is super humiliating. The thing I am the most embarrassed of, that I left up on YouTube just for my students, is the thing that all these successful artists that I'll be working with in California will associate me with, and they'll think that is the level that I'm at.* It was as though time itself stood still for me and I'll never forget how it felt.

For the first time in my life, deep overwhelming embarrassment was there, but I was somehow okay with it. It was okay that the people I was hoping would be impressed by me got to see the absolute worst I had to offer before meeting me. I remember sitting in my disbelief and stunned silence for a good twenty minutes, thinking, *Huh. This is humiliating. Wow. Well, there it is then,* and feeling this weird duality of peace and embarrassment at the same time. It was a unique moment of reflection, and I tried to find some lesson in it for myself besides the voice in my head screaming, *I told you that you should have taken that song down, Heidi!!* I still think about that instance and wonder what its purpose was in my life. I don't have any answers other than it was the first time I was really embarrassed to my bones, but it didn't matter. **When fear of embarrassment falls off, the wings can spread for flight.**

My next student, Kate, is heading for flight now and just saved up enough money herself for a laptop and recording equipment so she can begin self-producing her amazing songs. I mean this girl is young but can Write. A. Song. However . . . I remember the first year of lessons where she cried in every lesson the whole year. I don't even think she sang for me for the first couple lessons, just cried. I think even the second year might have been the same. Sometimes that's how long it takes to rearrange headspace. If she wasn't so freakishly musical, I think I would have suggested we end lessons, but her musicality and potential were through the roof. Here she is to tell you how she got from tears to flight.

Kate's Story:

"The first lesson I had with Heidi was very scary for me. Music is one of my favourite things, but something was stopping me from doing a lot of things with it. I was writing good songs, but I didn't share them with anybody. When I first began learning anything new with Heidi, I would begin to panic the second I didn't know how to do something or when I made a mistake. There were millions of negative thoughts racing through my head. I was afraid Heidi was judging me or that I was failing the lesson or not smart enough, so my first reaction would be to panic. PANIC!!!!! I couldn't stop myself. Almost immediately, tears would rush down my face, and I would run for the Kleenex box. When I started crying (which happened almost every lesson), I started thinking that Heidi would also think bad things about me because I was crying like a baby and couldn't stop. Honestly, the smallest things you could think of made me panic. I had many, many crying sessions. If any of you out there are in the same situation, you'll get through it if you just try. After a long crying session, many almost-tries, and taking risks, it will get you somewhere. I swear, I cried many lessons in a row, but somehow, after taking the fifty risks that Heidi prompted us to do, after a while, it slowly diminished. The more I got used to taking them and doing the things that I was not perfect at, the less I was scared.

"She also began to take ten minutes at the beginning of each lesson to teach me something that was too advanced for me at my skill level. It was a game to see whether I could keep calm while failing at something for ten minutes and keep myself from crying. Because she made it into a game, and I hate losing at games, I looked forward to that challenge each week and didn't realize that at the same time, I was training my brain not to panic when learning something I didn't understand and showing process to someone. I have not cried this year in lessons yet. Instead, I have been singing and trying new things now for a long time without crying or worrying.

"My first reaction to trying anything new used to be to panic, and then cry. But now, I welcome new things, and I honestly feel very proud of myself when I do something I could never have done a few years ago. So, if you ever worry about making mistakes or trying new things in your life, remember that once you start showing process, and the more you get used to being a little embarrassed, no matter the number of tears, it will work out, and eventually you won't sit in lessons with Kleenex boxes. You might even spend one trying, laughing at all of your mistakes with your teacher, and learning something."

Another great story about overcoming embarrassment comes from my former student Alex, who came to me for singing lessons because she had been given a solo in a musical and had no singing experience. We had a short amount of time to get her show ready, and the first night didn't go exactly as we planned it would . . .

Alex's Story:

"I remember my very first performance in my school musical onstage. It was my first time singing in front of people in a long time, and the thing I was most scared about was getting a voice crack onstage. The first note that I had to hold by myself, I got a voice crack that was really, really bad. The thing is, nothing stopped. The song kept going. I had to keep singing. People still clapped and came to congratulate me afterward. That was the worst thing that I could have ever imagined happening, and it didn't matter. The world kept turning. That experience changed me as a performer. I am not afraid to go out onstage and try something anymore because I failed, and it didn't matter that much."

While I think training and growing in your chosen art form is absolutely essential, equally valuable is displaying your process while you are growing. A year or two in hiding can easily become five or ten. It is often harder to break out of that pattern once you have been hiding for a long time. If you struggle in this area, do not believe the lie that it is hopeless. Look at the other voices who have pushed through—if they can do it, so can you. There is nothing stopping you! Your assignment is to display something authentic and imperfect once a week on your social media account, or send it to someone you trust if that's too scary a start. Let them see you frustrated, working, failing, trying, succeeding. Let them see you exactly where you are on your journey. That will help free you up a little bit so that you can start taking larger risks. You have nothing to prove, only to share. If you need some encouragement, head over to my heidikortesmusicstudio Instagram and watch one hundred of our bloopers.

MINDFUL MEDITATION:

"I am safe to be me in this world. I connect with my heart and know I am wanted and greatly loved. I accept and receive from life experiences. I embrace my learning process. I have all that is required to move forward. I move forward."

CHAPTER SUMMARY:

- Embarrassment isn't the end of the road for you.
- Showing process helps you grow in authenticity.
- Showing process also helps combat rigid perfectionism.

QUESTIONS TO PONDER:

1) Do I allow others into my process?
2) Do I share my art with people, my family? If not, what am I waiting for?

NOTES:

_____
_____
_____
_____
_____
_____
_____
_____

CHAPTER 11
SELF-DISCIPLINE

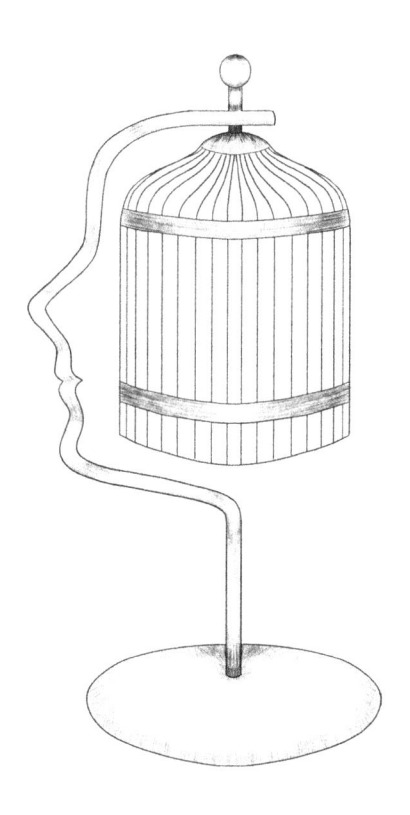

"Until you value yourself, you won't value your time. Until you value your time, you will not do anything with it.[11]*"*

M. Scott Peck

Out of all the obstacles, self-discipline is perhaps the trickiest one for a teacher to remedy in a student because we are not at home with them and can't walk with them through their week. The choice and decision to work on their own is up to them. Sometimes, it's laziness that keeps a student from growing, but other times it's these legitimately important things that pull on them and gobble up all their time. For instance, I know that if my students are out every night with their families, or have jobs after school, it's almost impossible for them to fit in a regular practicing schedule. No practicing means very slow improvement and oftentimes a lot of guilt and self-blame, which we will address later on.

There is also a certain type of student I have encountered, often really naturally talented and gifted, that just doesn't want to put in the effort even though they have the time. Confession: this was me in high school in my piano lessons. I would frantically 'cram-practice' a half an hour before lessons to try to make it seem like I had practiced all week. I went into lessons with a big, fun personality to try to distract my teacher from finding this out. News flash: I'm pretty sure she knew and was probably sighing inwardly during most of my piano lessons.

Sometimes I do succeed at motivating a lazy student to work on their own steadily, but whether I do or not often depends on how much they want a career in music someday. If you want to be a backup dancer for J.Lo, you have to be working out and dancing every day to get those abs of steel needed for that kind of job. There needs to be a certain unwavering drive about you and daily improvement of your skill. If this component is missing, no matter how brilliant you are, there will be a ceiling to how far you progress in your art. Other people who maybe do not have as much raw talent might achieve the exciting things that you are after because they are dedicated and so full of self-discipline. I am not saying this to shame you, just being honest.

For the first five or six years of teaching, I did not practice. I was far enough ahead of all my students that there was no need for my self-improvement. Teaching was becoming mundane and boring for me because I was teaching the same foundational things over and over again. I remember feeling highly dissatisfied, like my life was over, and thinking to myself, *Is this it? Am I just living for the students now? Is there nothing left in life for me?*

What ended up happening next was I came across the band Postmodern Jukebox, and I discovered there were many singers my age doing the things I wanted to do. Somehow that gave me the gumption to start growing again. I started taking jazz piano lessons with a local Winnipeg jazz artist, vocal lessons from a studio in California, and began learning bass, guitar, drums, and music production. Music came alive again. I came alive again. The plateau is something you really want to avoid. When you are on the plateau of being at the same skill level for too long, your love of your craft can become uninteresting and unsatisfying. A common practice for me is to look back after a month and ask myself what I have learned or improved upon. Anything? As an adult in the workforce who is not a full-time creative, I try to learn at least one new thing a month, minimum.

A couple of students that I am thinking of right now have big dreams for their music. They are amazing songwriters, great singers, and great communicators on stage. But these beautiful humans only work on their craft on their lesson days, cramming in a ton of work to cover up the fact that during the week, nothing was done. This is okay when you are in lessons and not in the professional world (I mean, it's still not ideal), but in the professional art world, you will need to have the ability to work on your own when you start to get paying jobs. Clients will want deadlines met, and that means that you will need to be on task with whatever you've been hired to do. If you are constantly late, last minute, or rush the job, people will not want to work with you as much as someone who shows up prepared with their best effort and a good attitude. As someone who has sat on audition panels, if it is a choice between taking the lazy performer who's more talented or the performer who is less talented but works twice as hard, I will always choose the hard-working one who shows up prepared.

As you can probably imagine, problems with daily practicing are not a unique thing. After teaching for ten years, if I had a dime for every time I have said "Did you practice this week?" . . .

The next four students have been in and out of that "I just can't get my practicing together" club, and all of them for different reasons.

Bren's Story:

"Practicing has never been a strong suit for me. I think some of that comes from me being a procrastinator, but another part could also be that I am an impatient person and don't see fast enough results right away with a few short practice sessions. I don't feel the drive to practice at all because sometimes the improvement is so slow. I'm blessed to be very naturally talented musically and was born into a family that sang and toured together as a musical group. Often, I didn't feel like I needed to practice because growing up I never had to; I'm able to pick things up as I go and figure them out on the fly without much work. This is a major benefit and also a downfall. I think sometimes the confidence that comes with being smart and naturally gifted can stop someone from getting to the next level. Growing up, I was used to acing tests without studying or performing well when I hadn't really practiced at all. I have a head for catching on to things quickly by simply watching someone do something. This is a good and a bad thing because it means I can afford to be lazy because I can get it without much effort. A few times I've tried teaching myself an extremely complex electric guitar solo, but then after half an hour gave up because it was going to take too much time, and I'd rather be doing other things. Or I just got frustrated and walked away. Because the majority has come easily to me in music, it is easy for me to drift and not improve to the next level.

"Heidi, who has continually called me out on this lack of practicing, has taught me that working regularly does make a difference over time (even though I still have a really hard time just doing it). I have learned some complex jazz chords in the last year that I am super proud of and have also learned a new instrument."

Cailin's Story:

"Motivation is an important and vital piece of life that can sometimes be overlooked— though we cannot really get things done without it. I have loved music all my life, although I admit that I have gone through phases where playing and practicing were not enjoyable. I started participating in group classes from a very young age and really enjoyed the fun and expressive sessions—singing, dancing, and playing basic instruments. I liked the energy of learning with other kids, found the theory and knowledge good, and the teacher was nice. I completed the program and continued taking private piano lessons with the same teacher. I enjoyed my private lessons as well, but I found that over time I grew tired of the rigidity. I found that practicing became much more of a chore than fun. I eventually decided to stop playing. That was not the right answer as I missed music in my life. I realized that for me, music didn't have to be so structured, and I needed to find the joy in music again. The way I rediscovered that joy was in finding my love for singing. I found wonderful teachers in a studio where I could learn how to play music that I wanted to play, which allowed me to foster my love for music and enjoy playing piano again. In the meantime, I learned to write songs, which was a great outlet for everything that I was going through as it allowed me to process my emotions and experiences and grow as a person. I am still growing and developing my songwriting while also getting better at adding the music component. Posting my videos on the studio Instagram and participating in the "Opening Up" waitress music video has helped me build my confidence and overcome fear. I have come a long way on my musical journey. I still have a long way to go, but I am excited about music again. I want to make a difference with my music by continuing to write and record more songs. Changing the focus and style of my learning allowed me to regain my motivation and foster my love for music. My connection with music has been especially helpful in coping with the pandemic, and I am grateful for that."

Here are the words to one of Cailin's poems on the subject . . .

HEIDI KORTE

Wasting Time

When and how did I get so good at wasting time?
Some people might say I'm wasting theirs, like
my dad when I'm in always late for things which he hates,
my teacher when I'm too busy trying to make human connections in their
class than listening to them rabble on about history,
but the one I'm most worried about is my own.
Why and how am I so insistent on stopping myself from succeeding?
Even when I set goals in the morning, I find every excuse of other things
I have to do to stop myself from completing them.
I only showered yesterday, but I guess I need one again.
I can't eat without watching tv, oh no, that would be a shame.
Looks like Mom needs some help, let's not tell her what I have to do
and help her instead, what is wrong with me?
Maybe I'm just too afraid of the questions, can I really do it?
Am I good enough?

Eithne's Story:

"So, practicing. Or rather, not practicing, and the weekly struggle of desperately trying to master a piece of music in the seconds before a music lesson or band practice. Despite doing music lessons for over seven years now, I still struggle a lot with a lack of motivation to practice in between weekly music lessons and to practice for other endeavours like band class. It's obvious that in order to improve your playing, you have to actually practice, but I still have this daily war with myself: 'I should really practice now . . . but I just don't want to . . . oh well, I can always do it tomorrow,' and so I end up putting it off until the minute before I have to play a certain piece in my lesson. I procrastinate with many things in my life, and so, with music too, I have learned how to rush through it and act as if I have been working on it all week, but of course I haven't, so I end up having to relearn a piece that I spent all of last week's lesson learning as well. As you can see, procrastinating with practicing is a big waste of everyone's time (and my lesson) because what is the point of learning something just to have to learn it all over again next time, and perhaps even the time after that? In the past, I have gone sometimes months without practicing in between lessons, and though I hate to admit it, sometimes I still go several weeks without practicing. However, I am improving with motivating myself and practicing because I actually do enjoy playing my instrument. It's just the struggle to actually sit down and practice that's specifically hard for me. Thankfully, I have the opportunity to perform on a regular basis with Pass the Performance. The impending threat of having to play for more than one person is a great motivation to get myself practicing."

Sage's Story:

"Finding the motivation to practice has been one of my main causes of feeling overwhelmed, drained, and having an overall lack of passion. My negative outlook on practicing has followed me through from a very young age. It started to become very apparent as I became more and more involved and dedicated to my music making. I remember a specific lesson with Heidi, when I had been in a practicing slump for a few weeks in a row, and she said to me, 'This wasn't just a bad week. You haven't had a good practice week in a while.' Although I didn't want to admit it, I knew she was right. She encouraged me to acknowledge that there was an underlying issue that we needed to solve. This was a hard activity for me. I couldn't quite pinpoint why I was unmotivated or lacking inspiration, I just knew that I was. We made a list of feelings that I had toward practicing and what thoughts had been running through my head. I knew that these negative thoughts and feelings had to be changed in order to feel the passion that I wanted to feel again. It was very difficult to put into words what I was feeling and why I was feeling those things, but we made a list anyway. It wasn't detailed, and it was quite sparse. During this activity, I remember Heidi telling me, 'These sort of breaks or slumps usually happen before a breakthrough.' Having the positive outlook that *maybe something will come from this* was enough to inspire, engage, and relight the flame of passion that had been flickering out. Soon after that, I was writing songs and finding joy in my artistry and music making again. It is amazing how much of a role your mindset and perspective play on your motivation and drive.

"When I started studying classical percussion in my first year of university, I experienced a similar struggle in regards to practicing, motivation, and perspective. There were a ton of big changes happening in my life and all of a sudden, I was expected to pull up my socks, take a deep breath, and jump right in. Learning how to practice efficiently and effectively was key. It took time. There were a lot of days where I hardly practiced at all and others that were filled with accomplishments and improvement. I slowly got into a better routine and discovered when I practiced best. Figuring out what time of day you are most focused and productive is important as well as learning various strategies for how to approach practicing. Even as I found my 'groove' (pardon the pun), I kept running into a lack of motivation and focus. I found it very difficult to know where to start, and when I did figure it out, I wrestled with staying on task. I came to realize that it was alright if I didn't stay within the plans that I had made. As one of my good friends and fellow percussionists likes to say: 'Slightly better is better than not better at all.' Sometimes straying from the plan and the goal set out is okay. Putting too much pressure on yourself is unhealthy and can cause more problems in the end, so I've learned to ride the wave and keep paddling.

"Although straying from the plan is okay, I have found it helpful to have goals, whether they are small daily wants, weekly 'to-dos,' or bigger monthly desires. It is important to use these as guidelines and not get too caught up in them, but they can be useful for knowing where to start and having a bit of structure to practice sessions. I like to use time limits and set alarms for my goals. This approach makes the tasks seem less daunting and more attainable.

"Another strategy that my university percussion teacher suggested to me recently was to push a little bit further than my mind wanted to. During practice time, I would often get the feeling that I wanted to quit, or was tired, or simply did not want to practice anymore. She suggested using some sort of 'counters' (like coins or buttons) to determine when I was allowed to stop. Once I started to think, *I'm done for today*, or *I think I'll stop*, I brought out the counters and did whatever I was working on three to five more times (depending on how many counters there were). The purpose of this is to force you to go a little bit more than what you'd like so that you don't let your mind win. You fight the urge to give in to your inner thoughts."

> *"Creatives actually have to sit and start. If I am not writing, I am not a writer. If I'm not painting, I'm not a painter. Am I doing this? or am I not? That sounds harsh, but that's what it is. Keep at it. Plain and simple. You're not going to get well-crafted in your field if you don't do it."*
>
> **Natasha Boone – Canadian Author and Artist**

Something I like to do to coerce myself to grow if I am feeling lazy is commit myself to something in the public eye that will force me to practice. For example, this weekend I have committed to singing at a community market. I have spent the summer of 2020 starting this book, biking twenty-six kilometres a day, and working on soundproofing my car. I have not really touched my piano this month or been singing very much. Now that I have committed to a fifty-minute fully memorized set this weekend, my practicing is going to ramp up because I have created a space where I have no choice but to practice. I can either run away because I am feeling overwhelmed and be super embarrassed because of my lack of preparedness, or I can get to work and put the time in to get the job done. This does add a certain amount of nervous energy, and it might not be the ideal motivator, but it is something I use to snap myself out of a slump.

As an adult who doesn't have a teacher or someone to keep me accountable, it is easy for me to not practice and turn on the television instead. Really easy. Unbelievably easy. So creating these kinds of situations where I commit to something really forces that growth out of me. This summer, I decided very last minute that I wanted to shoot a cover music video for Patric Scott's "Haunted" inside an old run-down vaudevillian theatre in northern Ontario. The minute I had dancers agreeing to join me meant that I had now committed to being prepared with a backing track, costumes, fog machine, and storyboard in one week's time. The result? I worked my butt off getting a video ready because I didn't want to let my team down. Involving other people in my work also pushes me to be more excellent. **It is easier to do a sloppy job by yourself.**

When you are a student, your teacher creates these magical moments for you by entering you in dance competitions and music festivals and hosting recitals, open mic nights, art exhibitions, talent shows, etc. As a student, your fear level about participating in all these things might be pretty high, but (hopefully) these events motivate you to be prepared and to work extra hard. There will be moments as an adult, however, when you need to master the skill of creating these spaces for yourself so you can keep growing and creating. Maybe you make one YouTube video a month, or you start a website for selling your artistic creations and clothing designs. It involves risk, but the good thing is that if you also struggle with fear and are taking the fifty risks, these count toward those, and they will get you putting in creative time as well. Two birds, one stone. In all seriousness though, the ability to craft a situation where I am forced to grow has been really helpful for me.

So how much time should you be spending on your craft a day? Remember, the bigger the dream, the larger the time commitment to make it happen. So for all of you reading this book, the time invested each day might be different for each one of you. Off the top of my head, I would say if you are a beginner student and your art is your hobby, twenty to thirty minutes, five days a week is a good amount of time. If you are gearing toward a career in your field but are still in high school, forty-five to sixty minutes a day would be ideal. If you are out of school and trying to pursue a career in the arts, I would say upwards of two to three plus hours on your craft is a really good idea. For professionals, I would then say the time is still upwards of that because it also includes your marketing and promotion as well as your growth. It really depends on you and what your goals and dreams are. Just make sure that whatever time you allot for growing in skill, you stick to it!

MINDFUL MEDITATION:

> "I choose wisely. Wisdom is my companion. I choose to be focused on the task at hand unto completion. I take action. I choose abundance. I am empowered to completion. I am consistent as I grow in my gifting. I embrace life."

MOTIVATIONAL MOMENT:

> Take a look at your schedule and see if you can build in intentional regular time to work on your craft each week/day.

CHAPTER SUMMARY:

- Do everything you can to avoid the plateau.
- Try to learn at least one thing a month.
- Figure out how much time you should allot to your craft according to the size of your dream.
- Learn to create situations for yourself where growth is not optional.
- Including other people in your art often creates accountability and more commitment.

QUESTIONS TO PONDER:

1) How is my relationship with time?
2) Do I invest regular time each week toward my own craft? If not, what stops me?
3) Do I regularly meet deadlines?

NOTES:

CHAPTER 12
DISTRACTIONS AND TIME MANAGEMENT

It is so easy for me to get sucked out of reality and the things I want to achieve and into binge-watching Netflix or playing Candy Crush on my phone. (The number of times I have redownloaded Candy Crush, gone on a binge, and then deleted it off my phone is too many.) We are often pulled into hours and even days of playing video games, obsessively checking our social media, and watching way too much TikTok. The reels are the worst, eh? I love them, but cat reels on Instagram can eat hours of my life without me realizing it. Sometimes, as you will read later, other art forms can be used to inspire your creativity. But there is a line and **only you** will know for yourself what that line is. Something I am constantly weighing in on in my life is how much of it is spent in my **reality versus fiction.**

Only you will know if the media you are consuming is helping you be creative in your reality or allowing you to escape into a land of fiction to avoid your reality. When I get lost in a binge cycle of my favourite show for the umpteenth time, I can guarantee you it is not helping my art, it is not helping me achieve my goals, and it is absorbing time. It is dulling my senses and allowing my mind to relax. If you look at the most influential people in the world, I bet they have pretty amazing daily habits, and I can guarantee you that they do not binge five hours of television as a part of their day. Ouch. Even for myself writing this, it is ouch. I am not a master of this balance yet, so I personally try to use media to motivate myself to get projects done: for example, if I spend seven hours finishing this song, I will reward myself with one *Star Trek* episode. If you want to achieve really big things artistically with your life, it is logical to conclude that sacrifices will have to be made, and that you are going to need to keep your head in your reality and regulate how much fiction you put in. How is the fifteen hours of television I watched on a weekend beneficial to my dreams and goals?

Why are we drawn to lose ourselves in fiction so much? For me, it's sometimes that I don't want to deal with the more difficult things in my life, so I escape them by entering into a world where I don't have to be anxious or think about those things. One episode leads to twenty, and then my day is used up. Am I saying that entertainment is bad? No. I hope that's not what you're picking up from this. Entertainment is not bad. It's about balance. If you are using entertainment to inspire your own art, then I would even say it's helpful to you. Only you can be the judge there. The thing to keep in mind is that you only have one life. One life. One life. Someday that time will be used up, unless we unlock the secret of immortality and transfer our conscious minds into androids like in *Star Trek* . . . But assuming that doesn't happen in your lifetime, at the end of your life, do you want to look back and see twenty years of television on the couch or that you actually did the things you really dreamed you would? I tend to be drawn to the couch and to the video game, so I know that is a tendency I have to personally be hyper-aware of because it is a hindrance and almost never a help to me.

Many of my students struggle with procrastinating in practicing, or they will frantically put in practice hours the night before a lesson. My student Addi, who I am so proud of as she is in a beautiful place of courage and growth right now in her music, used to really struggle with putting things off whenever I would assign her something to work on.

Addi's Story:

"I procrastinate a lot. In fact, I've been procrastinating writing this paragraph for over a week now. I realize that I shouldn't be putting off my work for so long, but I finish most things on time, even if I do it all the night before. So I continue to procrastinate because I know it will be done eventually and that works well enough; however, it doesn't actually work well. At some point I'm going to miss an important deadline because of this, and I know that. Then why do I keep procrastinating? The longer I put off doing something, the more difficult it seems (even if it's a simple task like cleaning my room), and that makes me want to do it even less.

"Sometimes, I will decide to finally work on the thing that I need to … after one more TikTok. Of course, that one TikTok turns into an hour of pointless scrolling. I think the best way to stop procrastinating is to start without thinking about it too much. Starting is the hardest part, after all. Another thing that helps me to stop procrastinating is to imagine myself doing the task and enjoying it, then imagining how good I will feel once it's done. Obviously, procrastination is still something I'm trying to do less of, and I don't think it will ever be something that I never do at all, but if I work hard enough, I think I could get close."

The thing you will want to discover or create for yourself is a balance between work, entertainment, social time, and rest. **The size of your dream and the amount of effort required to achieve it will be what sets your balance between these four things**. I asked an international speaker who has authored many books how much media they watched in a day, and their answer was one hour. Gulp. I also just listened to a financially successful and powerful CEO talk about her routine, and she said she doesn't watch television at all. Double gulp. So even there we see the size of their dream affects that balance. Currently, I would say two hours of media would be a fantastically good day for me, including social media checking. Now, Siri tells me how much screen time I average a week, and well . . . it's very embarrassing! Let me say that one more time: **the size of your dream and the amount of effort required to achieve it will be what sets the balance between work, entertainment, social time, and rest.**

> *"Time is a currency you can only spend once, so be careful how you spend it."*
>
> *Harmon Okinyo* [12]

Natasha Boone – Canadian Artist and Author

"Distraction. I am highly distracted at all times. For instance, I will have five paintings on the go, three books I'm writing, my illustrations, and my illustration groups that I am a part of, etc. None of this is bad, it's just when I get to a point of being overwhelmed and flustered by all of them that I need to re-evaluate why I am reaching for distractions and not allowing myself to focus. I would say one of my biggest obstacles is focus. I always have a million ideas, which is good but also bad because I can get bogged down by the ideas and not end up finishing anything. My biggest challenge is crossing the finish line, completing something, putting my checkmark on it, and then moving on to the next thing.

"Honestly, how I overcome this is with discipline, which is not a fun word. A lot of being a creative involves discipline and self-awareness. At this point in my career, I am self-aware enough to recognize that I like to have lots of projects on the go, and that's okay, but I also need to finish some of those projects. It's the balance of allowing myself to have lots of ideas but also the discipline of needing to finish them. Practically speaking, I do this by having **an accountability partner.** For the book I wrote, every week I would email my accountability partner the chapter I had completed. She didn't even have to look at it, but emailing it to her was enough for me to meet my goals of writing a chapter a week and finishing my book. Another thing I like to do is build community around my projects and discuss my ideas with others. I dialogue and get feedback and motivation that way. Something that helps me with distractions and feeling overwhelmed at all my ideas is self-care. I know that's overused, but getting enough sleep, going for walks, exercising, and stabilizing myself as a person helps keep my creative life from getting out of whack."

A trick I can give you for helping get you on a regular training/artistic schedule is to create a monthly Excel chart for your wall and include all the things you want to get done in a day. The things that are of the utmost importance to you. You don't want to have too many of them because then you won't achieve them all and your self-esteem and drive might plummet as you fail to check off each box. Really. Make sure that you actually create achievable and realistic goals. On my chart currently are the seven or eight things I want and am able to achieve each day across the top—Exercise, Yard Work, Music, Writing, Spirituality, Cleaning, Lectures. Then vertically on the left-hand side, I have the numbers of the month going down the sheet. Every day, my goal is to check off as many of them as I can. I like getting check marks, and it gives me a sense of accomplishment to mark something off my list. That sense of achievement gives me motivation for the next day. The chart also gives me direct feedback if I am dropping the ball in an area. If I look at the last fifteen days and see that I didn't clean my bathroom once, then it's time to make a change! And also . . . ewwww. If you need some structure and organization to your days so you don't spend them in distraction, get out some paper and get that chart made! If I accomplish everything I set out to do in a day, then I get a media reward. I also usually assign an amount of time to each activity too, that way I don't spend seven hours cleaning and missing out on all the other things I wanted to work on that day. This is just one of the ways you can motivate yourself. The way I do it now is a bit more organically, but when I was in a slump, seeing my goals on the wall really helped.

One of the big flaws in my personal time management on a day off was that I would make a colossal list of things I wanted to accomplish. It would have way too many things on it for one day. Then I would sit there in the morning looking at it, stressing about which one to start first and how I was going to get the list all done. Hours and hours later, I would still be on the couch stressing about which thing on my list I should do first. Literally just sitting there stressing myself out. On a day like that, there would be some point where I would give up on the day and begin to watch television to avoid feeling awful about myself and to avoid the list that I was so excited about knocking out of the park just a couple hours earlier. I have written multiple songs about this problem that I have not yet produced. Here are the beginning lyrics to one of them:

> *Another day, can't make a decision.*
> *That's the time my life starts spinning.*
> *Retreating from the tornado in my mind.*
> *Who'd have thought it could get like that with my free time.*
> *So I sit on my couch, I feel dizzy.*
> *Long list to do, but I'm not getting busy.*
> *After a while looking for something to numb my mind.*
> *T.V. will do the trick.*
> *The list is untouched, I feel sick.*

What can you glean from my struggle? It's important when setting up your daily goals that you make them manageable and also leave room for the unexpected. Have realistic expectations of what you can accomplish in a day, and just start! All the time you spend thinking about what you are going to do is time you aren't doing it!

MINDFUL MEDITATION:

"I choose reality. I embrace my path to my artistic expression. I have an abundance of inspiration. I choose to be focused. I am full of anticipation to see my future unfold. I engage with inspiration and see clearly. I am in touch with my purpose as I centre myself in my heart."

MOTIVATIONAL MOMENT:

Go spend an uninterrupted hour on your craft. Learn something new if you can.

CHAPTER SUMMARY:

- Balancing work, entertainment, social time, and rest is important.
- The balance will depend on the size of your dream.
- Keeping your feet in your reality is important—only you will know if you are using media to foster creativity or to escape from it.
- To get into a routine, try making an Excel sheet with your goals for each day on it and space to check off whether or not you did each goal.
- Make sure to set realistic and achievable goals so that motivation stays high.

QUESTIONS TO PONDER:

1) What are some of the things that distract me and waste my time?

2) In my stage of life and with my goals for my craft, how much time is a good amount for me to invest regularly in it?

NOTES:

_____
_____
_____
_____
_____
_____
_____

CHAPTER 13
AVOIDANCE

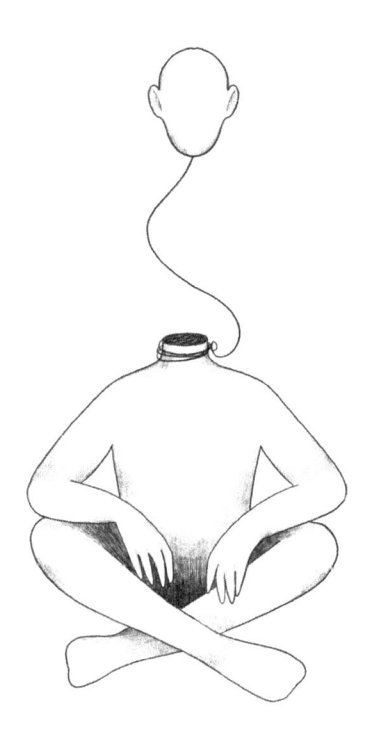

Sometimes people procrastinate in their art form because they are lazy or distracted, but sometimes they avoid practicing or working on a project because of the simple fact that they are feeling overwhelmed by it. This was a little more me. Not so much anymore, but I used to be a hardcore avoider of anything that seemed too big or scary for me to handle. When I was in my twenties, I would check the mail and see a phone bill that I couldn't pay. I would take out all the other mail but leave the bill in the mailbox for weeks and weeks. Somehow, if I didn't open it up, it wouldn't really exist, and I was safe from facing it. Terrible idea. Don't do it. That might seem really silly, but it was a real thing for me, and it never worked out well. When we believe that we can't handle something, we usually run from it. I guess the question is, is that belief actually true? Or are you just listening to the irrational fear monster?

I have a couple of students who avoid because of fear regularly, and a lot of students who do this only occasionally. I would address the mind first. Why do you feel helpless? Why do you feel overwhelmed? What are the thoughts in your mind saying? The reason behind feeling overwhelmed is sometimes a hard one to diagnose and push through because there could be multiple reasons for why you are feeling that way, and only you can be the judge of what it is and what your course of action should be. For my student Lanae, it was that pesky comparison telling her she will never be good enough that caused her to avoid growing on piano. Here is a snippet of her journey.

Lanae's Story:

"My biggest mental block when it comes to music so far has been avoidance. I've been trying to get better at improvising, but I seldom do it. Pretty much since the beginning, I have associated improvisation with feelings of guilt and disappointment, which has made me avoid it because I don't like feeling that way. During one of my Zoom lessons where I had not practiced, we actually called up another student who had also struggled with lack of motivation at one point and just talked with her. She asked me what my 'why' was—what I was trying to achieve by playing the piano or getting into music. Not only was that a much bigger question than I had considered, but because of that question, I figured out why I wanted to get better, and it helped me gain a desire to improvise. I began setting reminders on my phone, and I put up visual representations of what I'm doing it all for. I also struggle with comparison, just as many others do. I tend to forget that the same people that I compare myself to were once at the same level as me. Personally, I think that this plays into my avoidance because as I sit down to improvise, my mind replays all the beautiful things I've heard my friends play, and I allow my mind to discourage myself. Then I start thinking about how I won't ever measure up. I'm super proud of myself for getting better at quieting the intrusive and diminishing thoughts that I have, and I am now enjoying showing process a lot more. I still have a long way to go before I am where I want to be, but I'm farther than when I started, and that makes me happy."

Sometimes when we are piling on too much in our life, working too hard, and feeling stressed to the max, there is a breaking point where everything becomes overwhelming. The solution to this kind of overwhelmed is not so easy and involves letting some things go in your life. I will talk about strategies to handle that in the next chapter. First, I want to discuss how feelings of being overwhelmed happen because of **panic and lie-based thinking**. In this instance, you would be avoiding a project because you think you are going to fail at it or you don't know where to start.

I suggest setting a small, time-based goal for working on your project. Setting timers really helps me begin something overwhelming because I can tell my brain that I only have to deal with being overwhelmed for fifteen minutes. Set your timer and do fifteen minutes of work on your project. When the timer goes off, walk away from it, and then don't think about it again that day. Then do that the next day and the next. What I usually find as I settle into a creative project I have been avoiding is that the anxiety comes way down as I look around and see that it's not going as bad as I had envisioned it going, once I get my feet moving. That is pretty much how I coax myself to do anything I am overwhelmed with nowadays. In writing this, I am preaching to myself as I have been asked to run a vocal workshop for three hours next week in a COVID-19 mask, to children in masks, ages seven to fifteen. Right now, fear is saying, "Yikes, this is going to be a disaster in masks, especially when the age range is great. You will be eaten and spit out by these kids like Jonah and the whale." And there could be some element of truth to this because of the age range of the students and the pandemic policies (break from writing). I actually just took my own advice and texted a theatre guru who's taught groups in a mask through the pandemic to help me plan the workshop. Sometimes it's just about that first baby step that sets your project in motion. Further disclaimer, it actually went really well and the singers I worked with were absolute sweethearts—it was definitely more difficult in masks but nothing like what fear was yelling at me. It's like I am writing this book for me or something...

So an absolute must, especially when in tasks that feel overwhelming and that you want to avoid for fear of them going poorly, is the transition to thinking of **time invested** instead of **task completed**. In your creative time, I highly recommend this way of thinking especially when you are working on larger projects that cannot be accomplished in one day. People who are task driven in their practicing consider two hours of work a failure if the task is left incomplete and often get frustrated much quicker because of their inability to complete it within a pre-envisioned timeframe. I have leaned toward being task focused most of my life, which worked well as long as it was a project I could accomplish quickly. Let's say, though, that I have a task that I want to accomplish in music production, like recording a piano track, and something goes wrong with my gear, there is a crackling noise, or I am unable to get good sound going into my computer to even begin the process of recording the piano. I end up spending two hours fixing that and troubleshooting, and I don't even get to the task I really wanted to accomplish that day. Current Heidi would say, "I won today, and I am two hours closer to being done," because I put in the time I had set aside for my art. Even though the task I had initially intended to accomplish never even got started, I would still say that I achieved something because I would be two hours closer to getting something done. I tell my students that as long as they are putting in daily time, I don't care if they accomplish anything I assign them in a week or not (gasp!). In fact, most often their 'to-do' lists from me each week are way too long anyways. If my students tried to get all the tasks done that I threw at them in a week, they might panic and avoid working altogether because they feel overloaded by me. But because they (should) know that what I care about is time invested, I don't perceive any stress from them in this area. Make sense? Of course, there will be moments when you need to be focused on completing a task that has a deadline, like learning a routine for a dance audition or a play's performance or preparing for an art exhibition, but I think that in general, day-to-day life, greater success often results from a steadiness of time put in. **You are running a marathon, not a sprint.**

This concept of 'time invested' vs. 'task finished' is also helpful when you have something that you keep failing at, like me learning a triple pirouette...

or even a single one . . . the struggle is real. Having the mindset of 'time invested' will help you to keep a calm head and not panic, get depressed, or give up. You spent your one hour working on your pirouette and didn't get it yet, but you still spent the one hour dedicated to your art. You win! In your future field, sometimes things will not go your way and you will need to be ready to be able to handle that emotionally, guard your positivity, and keep your forward motion happening. When you lose that, you lose. Having a time goal will help you feel like you accomplished your mission for the day.

Sometimes I have assigned a student something I knew they would fail at for the week just to test them and see if they can keep their positive outlook. I only do this test once with senior students who are stable, as my first or second years aren't ready to handle that emotionally. The senior students usually pass this test with flying colours, which is always a proud teacher moment. In their future careers, whatever they may be, the ability to think clearly and refuse to give up after failing multiple times is super valuable. So, think of your task each day with your craft as 'time.' If you invest the time, you've accomplished your task. Onward.

MINDFUL MEDITATION:

> "I am enough. I am safe. I am inspired as I take action. I embrace small beginnings as I focus my energy. I am enough. I have all that I require to release my creative expression. I am creativity. I follow my dream."

MOTIVATIONAL MOMENT:

> Take a project that you have been too afraid to start and spend fifteen minutes beginning it. Then, if you still have time left in your day, go on a walk and get some fresh air.

CHAPTER SUMMARY:

- Set a timer for projects you are too afraid to start.
- For bigger projects, begin to use time goals instead of task-based ones.
- You are running a marathon, not a sprint.
- Sometimes just starting something scary makes it less scary.

QUESTIONS TO PONDER:

1) Do I avoid? If so, what are the thoughts behind my avoidance? How can I replace them with empowering thoughts?

NOTES:

_____
_____
_____
_____
_____
_____
_____

CHAPTER 14
RUSHING TO GET THE JOB DONE

The other side effect of being too task-oriented is rushing a project to complete it and ending up with a sloppy job. This is still another big one for me, so maybe I am writing these two chapters just for myself. I am someone who dreams big, starts a project full steam ahead, and then gets very impatient once I have put in a certain number of hours (usually around forty). At that point in my project, I stop liking my own music and just want it to be 'done' at all costs. I rush wildly to the finish line to get it completed by tomorrow 'at the latest.' Is there anyone else reading this who is like this? I sure hope I am not the only one. I don't know that I have any students who are like this, but I believe I can't be the only one.

May I just say that this NEVER works out in my favour, as the end result is almost always sloppier and I find mistakes later on. I think I am slowly getting better at this, but this would still be my very weakest element. When I feel 'done' with something and ready for the next project, my tendency is to race to finish it so I can be on to the next thing that I suddenly feel passionate about. Almost like starting a new romance for some people. I tend to be able to focus on only one thing at a time instead of juggling five or six projects like some of the greats do. Something I am going to try to help me not race out of a project is having a couple of projects on the go at one time. This way there is more creative energy, and I don't get bored, tired, or frustrated of being stuck in one project that feels like it is taking forever. Involving other people also helps curb the desire to finish it in a rush. Like I mentioned earlier, when other people are involved in my art, I take extra care to make sure it's good because I don't want them to regret being part of it.

Something else I recommend doing is hiring out some of the jobs for your projects by using Patreon. If you've never heard of it, as of the year 2022, Patreon is incredibly helpful for artists trying to raise funds for projects. It is a subscription service where your patrons get rewards and perks for supporting you financially. With my patrons' help, I am able to save myself from weeks of editing on my already hour-heavy projects. I usually record all the instruments for my songs myself so by the time audio and video editing come around, it feels really long. Also, side note: some of my most meaningful memories of my work so far have been my interactions with other people. Involve people whenever you can!

A former student of mine, music producer and recording artist Dane Bjornson, and I had a chat about rushing to get a project done. We both have struggled with rushing, but he rushes for a different reason than I do. He rushes because he doesn't allow himself the proper amount of time or margin for the unexpected to happen. Here is one of his latest rushing stories for you.

Dane Bjornson – Music Producer, Recording Artist

"It was finals week, and I was taking a course with one of my favourite professors in production school, and I had a full track due that Friday to present to him. I wanted to have a really good showing for this person. He liked to work with really great musicians, so I had decided that's what I would showcase. I was working three days a week and trying to wrap everything up with school at the same time. I showed him what I had on Monday, and I planned to record vocals, harmonies, write lyrics, and mix by Friday. I left myself two hours to mix the song. I can do an okay mix in two hours, but my computer program decided not to like any of my technology, and it crashed. I had to bus to work that night, and because I couldn't do anything more, I just had to export the song as it was. Even though it was academia, and I was paying to fall flat on my face, that was probably one of the least proud moments of my musical career. I ended up getting a good mark on it, but I just know the mix sounded not good. I was so stressed and was rushing hard. I had overcommitted myself, and I didn't start working on that project until a week and a half before the deadline, but he had given us the assignment a month earlier.

"I am starting to avoid rushing deadlines now in the professional world. Whatever deadline I give a client, I put it two weeks earlier in my calendar, just to mess with my own scheduling and brain about it. Making to-do lists has also been huge for me."

My student Carrick started taking lessons with me around age eight. He has a remarkable memory and intelligence level, but his biggest enemy was impatience. At that age, his mind craved learning new things, but the repetition involved in gaining that new skill was almost too much for him to handle. For him, it was age that remedied this problem. (Wish it was the same for me lol.) Here are his words.

Carrick's Story:

"When I was just starting piano, I couldn't finish anything. I wasn't patient enough. I wanted to do the next song because I had done the one I was working on enough, and it sounded good enough to me. In reality, it did not. I still have a binder full of unused half choruses and songs I never finished. I overcame it by growing up. I still don't like the sound of me going too slow, but I think I've really conquered that one in music now."

Leaving margins is one of the solutions to the people who rush because they didn't leave time for the unexpected to happen. Someone in my life who has really helped me with the concept of leaving a margin is Wendy Peter. I remember sitting in one of her talks in a class I was taking, and she was super strict. She told us we had to text her if we were going to be even five minutes late for the class. I asked Wendy to talk a little bit about that for you.

Wendy Peter – Author, Speaker, Teacher

"Margins are important because they are your gift to yourself. **When you create a margin in your life, you establish what matters to you**. When you don't create space for what matters to you, you allow the tyranny of the urgent and other people's expectations to dictate what you do with your time. Value margins. **To value creating margins and creating space is to value yourself, your soul, and the place creativity springs from.** Think of it as self-care. It's also the ability to hold longevity in your career. You can burn up and burn out or you can have sustainability. To have sustainability, you must learn not to overdo it.

"Having margins means that you live life in such a way that you create an internal hierarchy where you define what matters, and you give space and place to those things. **You define what matters and what you need to actually matter yourself.** Your rest needs to matter and even leisure needs to matter because as a creative, the soul is what brings forth creativity. When we give rest to our soul by giving margins around us by saying no to things that are too much for us, we actually create space for our soul to come alive and create. This is what I need to be my best self. I am not going to be a desperate person who says yes to everything, abuses my body, or works harder than I should. I think of the word **unhurried** and think creatives could learn a lot from studying it.

"I think it's also a really great idea to not allow having to deliver a deadline be the motivating factor in getting you to complete your work. Too many people allow that to be their only motivation. What that does is actually teaches you to respond to fear and pressure rather than to create out of love and rest. I write books, and I create a publishing deadline for myself that is a **full month before** the publisher wants them. I also set up a **reasonable goal**, which is that I am going to write a chapter each month. I work on one chapter for a period of time. This allows me to leave it and come back to it. It also allows me to say we are going to conclude this chapter by such and such a date. Some people have to schedule their practice time and that's what works for them. For a highly creative person, that can feel like punishment, but if you don't have the discipline of practice, nothing gets done. I think for creatives who find themselves in that place, **you actually want to create deadlines that give you space.**"

Sitting down with Wendy always leaves me in a deep ocean of thought. What she said about creatives' motivation being because of deadlines instead of rest has really challenged my own thinking in this area. I would have to say that currently, it is having a deadline that inspires me to create a lot of the time. But perhaps as Wendy said, there is something better for us.

MINDFUL MEDITATION:

"I move forward in perfect timing. I am flexible as is required to give my best. I complete my task in fullness. I allow creativity to bloom in its fullness. I am balanced and centred. I move beyond my perceived limitations. I enjoy giving the time required to finish well."

CHAPTER SUMMARY:

- Look for ways to help yourself when you feel 'done' with a project.
- Instead of rushing a project, consider hiring out or involving other people.
- Allow yourself the proper amount of time to complete something well.
- With deadlines, practice leaving margin in case the unexpected happens, so you'll still have time to finish

QUESTIONS TO PONDER:

1) How do I tackle bigger projects? Do I avoid? Do I rush? Why?
2) Do I ever involve other people in my creativity?
3) Do I have a creative community?
4) Are deadlines my only motivation in creation? When do I create out of rest?

NOTES:

CHAPTER 15
SCHEDULE OVERLOAD

Next, I want to address all you beautiful creatives who say yes to everything and overload your schedules to the point of your own mental exhaustion and burnout. Sound familiar? I have met so many of you. So. Many. I am resisting the urge to shout out all the student names for the last ten years.

If you are avoiding your craft because your schedule is constantly overloaded, then let's take some time to roll out the calendar and see what you have going on that prevents you from spending time with your art. It might be a good moment to take a step back and consider balance, priorities, etc. Picture the things you need to get done in a day being like pieces of a pie chart. You only have so many slices in a day, and if you give all the slices away to other people, you can't expect your artistic projects or dreams to move forward. If you are unintentionally self-sabotaging by saying yes to everyone, then remedying this will involve saying goodbye to some of the unnecessary and learning to use the word no! You might be someone who is only a creative on the side, in which case your craft will be lower on the priority scale for you, and your first loves will take the majority of your time. In this book, I will assume that all you young creatives who are reading it want to make space for your craft.

One of the most freeing words is 'no.' I honestly love that word so much. It gives you control over your schedule to some extent and how you spend your free time. If you are an 'always have to say yes' person, the very first piece of advice I would give to you is to **never say yes in the moment**. I am going to share with you my secret trick phrase I used when I was younger and feeling pressured that allowed me space to think clearly about a decision. When somebody approached me with an opportunity that I was unsure of, I would say, "Wow, that seems like such a great opportunity. Thank you so much for asking me. But my calendar is at home, so why don't I go home tonight, take a look, and get back to you tomorrow on whether that's a possibility or not?" Then when I was home, and not feeling pressured to please that person, I would do this exercise. I quieted myself down, closed my eyes, and held out both hands in front of me on my lap. In my right hand, I pictured myself saying yes to that opportunity. I looked ahead at the year with my imagination, and then I paid careful attention to how my stomach and body reacted. Then I turned toward the other hand with the 'no' and closed my eyes, and I pictured my year without that opportunity and imagined what it would look like in my mind, paying careful attention again to how my body reacted. I looked back and forth a couple times, right hand-left hand, yes-no, and almost always, my body was relaxed for one, and very tense for the other. This continues today to be how I make almost every scheduling decision in my life. If I just pay attention to what my own body, mind, and soul are saying, then hopefully I never get to the completely overwhelmed and burnt-out phase.

Now, years later, I am so aware of how I feel and what my limitations are, and I am very comfortable saying no on the spot to someone. Back when that was uncomfortable, I really needed that catchphrase so that I could think clearly about what adding one more thing to my schedule would do. Sometimes we don't listen to our intuition because we are afraid of disappointing people we respect. I tell my students that they are surely going to disappoint me at some point in our time together, and I might disappoint them as well. I like them to know that even when/if they let me down, I am still in their corner and rooting for them. With one student who was miserable because of his overcommitment to people, I actually asked him to commit to unreasonable things in lessons on purpose to help him practice saying no in a safe place. It was even hard for him to say no to me, but hopefully that practice got him ready for the real world.

If you have not been listening to your intuition, then it might be a bit of a process to untangle yourself from the unnecessary commitments that are wrapped around you. But as you begin to explore what is okay for you and what is not okay for you, I actually believe you will unlock new levels of joy and freedom in your life as you discover more about yourself and how to honour your feelings. I also would add that creativity definitely does not often flourish when there are time constraints and pressure. There needs to be empty space so that the mind can dream, imagine, and create.

We often know what is unnecessary, but we are just too scared to admit it. Many times, just quieting ourselves down and paying attention to what our intuition is telling us will let us know if something is good for us or not. If you have not learned this skill yet, this is a life changer.

Here is a story from a student who had too much to do in so little time.

Phoebe's Story:

"Growing up, music was an escape, and as cliché as it is, it's the truth. Put that together with the crazy hen house of eleven people that was my home for most of my adolescent years. Songwriting became a means to say exactly what I wanted to and how I wanted to say it. As much as I enjoyed the liveliness that my home contained, it also meant that I was responsible for more than I signed up for. What was once at the forefront of my entire being took a backseat to serve the needs of my family. I never thought I could lose my passion for music, but life can surprise you and pull you in a direction you never thought you'd go.

"Being the eldest in an immigrant family meant there wasn't enough space in my life to add music. It was an art form and not a job. That's the reality I was faced with. From bringing my grandma to doctor's appointments, taking my sister to dance class, and being a student with extracurriculars, music was just four steps out of reach.

"There was a time when I just felt like it was one more thing I needed to do, one more way to be pulled, stretched. For a time, it was asking me for too much. I didn't practice, no continuity or consistency was to be seen for a long while. It was probably like this for months or years, who knows. But as the saying goes, if you love something, let it go, if it comes back, it's yours forever. I didn't know if my opportunity for pursuing music was going to come back when I could manage it again, but I loved it enough to let it go for the time I couldn't give it my all.

"It's hard: if you've ever been heartbroken over something that was really wonderful, I'd say it has similar symptoms. You're left knowing how amazing it can be, but you know that what it requires isn't something you can give just yet. If your connection with your art truly runs deep, the instant gravitation toward it is hard to miss. It's a blaring alarm in your head that goes off every time you pass by your favourite instrument as it gathers dust in the corner of your room. As hard as it was being the sensible eldest child, the world moved on, and it was just me versus circumstance. That's when I figured it out at last—my love for music.

"Being on the brink of completely letting go is a distant memory now. Eventually, the need became far too loud as music's cries tugged on my heartstrings. Music couldn't continue being unnoticed, ignored, or brushed off to the side. There came opportunity after opportunity, and when I was ready to pick up the mantle again, they were waiting for me. You can't be afraid to dive back in because you're scared you might leave it again. If there's anything I've learned, it is that it's better to know when it's too much than to push yourself to the point of hating what you were once passionate about."

Like Phoebe, sometimes there are situations in life that will consume your schedule. As I write this paragraph, members of my immediate family have moved in together to take round-the-clock care of my mother. Between writing this book, taking care of her, and trying my hardest to be a fun, energetic aunt to my nieces and nephews, my own musical endeavours have been completely pushed to the side. Part of me is panicking and alarm bells are sounding inside of me because I feel there is just not enough time for what I love right now. But I am breathing through it and reminding myself: **There are seasons like this, and you have to bend with them. Your gift is not lost. Your creativity is not lost and will have its time to surface again after this season passes.**

MINDFUL MEDITATION:

> "I am content with what I am able to complete in a timely manner to my highest potential. I slow down and listen to my heart to be satisfied with what is mine to do and what is not. I know the difference. I love myself. I gift myself time to grow and expand in my ability. I embrace my fullest creativity. Time is my friend."

CHAPTER SUMMARY:

- Resist the urge to say yes to everyone.
- Make time in your schedule for creativity.
- Learn to listen to your intuition when scheduling yourself.
- Accept the things you cannot control, and bend with the seasons.

QUESTIONS TO PONDER:

1) How full is my pie chart?
2) How often am I at the brink of burnout?
3) Are there things I can let go of right now so that my art has a place to grow?
4) Am I comfortable saying no?
5) Do I listen to what my body is telling me?

NOTES:

_____
_____
_____
_____
_____
_____
_____

CHAPTER 16

THE LAND OF THE HALFWAY FINISHED PROJECTS

I polled some of my creative friends and asked them what their biggest artistic struggle was, and multiple people responded with half-finished projects, walking away before a job is finished. This is harder with projects that are paid while easier with ones that are your own and have no deadline or expectations from others. This obstacle has never really been something I personally struggle with, and when my students walk away mid-song, it irks me to no end. I think the solution to leaving things unfinished is to examine the reasons behind why you are stalled. I questioned some creatives in various fields who struggle with completing their works and asked them why, and these are some of their responses.

Haven Peckover – Canadian Visual Artist

"I think at first you get really excited about a project, and you spend eight hours on it, and then you leave it for months. Then you go back to it and wonder, *Why did I ever stop?* I think trying to prioritize your art becomes really hard because artists can often feel like they need to be more career driven. Making money, taking care of your home, your family, and all these other things, and then your passion kind of falls to the side a little bit. I have a painting that's been sitting for over a month and a half. It's the size of a postcard, and I still haven't finished it yet. My paying job involves art and the creative process, so I am still in tune with my creativity, but it's the thing that I love doing the most that often falls off of my track. I think as long as you do something creative every day, you feel like you are progressing in your craft. Big projects are intimidating, especially when you love something so much, so it kind of scares you to finish it. Even if it's just ten minutes every day of you doing what you want to do, then that can push you to spend more time increasing it to an hour, two hours, or a whole weekend working on a project."

Camille Meub – Writer, Upholsterer

"The closer to completion I get, the more I notice imperfections and get discouraged."

Shannon Schultz – Author, Painter, Watercolour Artist, Speaker

"I'm in the middle of at least four projects at this current time. I get started on a new painting, and it sparks another painting. I go back and forth between them, then over to a writing project. Now I have an embryo for another book, but an older book wants my attention, and now the painting is calling me back . . . acrylics or oils? Ah . . . and the video . . ."

Paige Uttley – Musician, Painter, Woodworker

"I struggle to finish my projects. They never look, sound, or function the way I intended them to, and so eventually I just give up on them because they all seem impossible!"

Jon Loeppky – Musician, Songwriter, Producer, Audio Engineer

"Finishing a project requires an incredible amount of discipline (or a reward) for me. Typically, the majority of projects I finish are either paid client work or a 'quick turnaround project' that I start and finish the same day. Everything else gets sidetracked by whatever new muse I find."

Let me tell you the very profound things that I do with my students. I remind them and pester them until they finish their projects, and ninety-nine percent of the time, that works. If you can find a way to make yourself accountable to someone or accountable online to your followers on social media, you will have people who know you have started something and who will be looking for the finished result.

For those who feel like Camille and Paige, learn to accept the imperfections in your work and still walk your projects to the finish line. You will (hopefully) learn from each project how to do the next one better. Present your completed project to someone ahead of you in your field and get critical feedback, that way you can grow your skill enough so that what is in your mind will eventually be accurately represented in your art. **An imperfect project is never a waste, there is always something to learn from it**. For you songwriters, poets, or scriptwriters, I tell my songwriting students to work on writing a completed song, not a good one. If they always focus on writing a first verse and a chorus but never a bridge or outro, their skill at writing the first half of a song will grow, but their bridges will most likely be weak because they have never practiced writing them.

If you are like my dear friend Shannon, juggling many projects at once, I am fascinated at your mind's ability to work like that and think it's great, as long as you eventually get your projects finished (which she does). That way of doing things is probably more exciting and fulfilling than what I do, which is plough through one big project until it is done. What I am trying to say to you is learn what you need to take a project from start to finish. Start to finish!

Jon Loeppky cont'd

"Last week, I bought a delay pedal off Marketplace for my electric guitar. I own a multi-effect pedal that has endless choices and parameters I can tweak to create the 'perfect sound.' The problem was all I ever did was tweak knobs. I never just played. It was an endless search for a 'better' setting. The Marketplace delay pedal only has a few knobs and no ability to tweak the tone. Do you want to know what happened? I started to play guitar again! For hours at a time, without stopping. I am being incredibly productive because of the choice to limit myself to a single pedal with minimal options. I am selling the multi-effects pedal soon so that I never go back to the land of 'creative potential' because that's all it provides. Potential. **Constraints are a creative's biggest blessing!** It's counterintuitive, but having boundaries and limits forces us to create solutions. Total freedom requires no creativity whatsoever; that untethered freedom is what makes many creatives unproductive."

Funny thing. Reading what Jon wrote here about constraints really helped me with writing my ten-minute Christmas musical for my nieces and nephew this year. Every Christmas they get a special ten-minute musical with their voices in it as the main characters and usually two or three original songs. I was pressed for time this year, so I decided to try Jon's advice out. I wrote my second song in the musical using only guitars and the third song with only vocal noises from my family. The limitations actually forced me to grow creatively as well as get moving. The result? A family solstice song that I am kind of in love with and releasing this year. Thanks, Jon!

MINDFUL MEDITATION:

"I have all that is required to move forward. I embrace the opportunity to complete what is in me to express. I focus my thoughts. I focus my energy. I complete my expression in a timely manner and am efficient in completing my goals. Others appear when I choose to have help. I rediscover my inspiration. I move with ease."

MOTIVATIONAL MOMENT:

Put down the book and spend thirty minutes today working on a project you've forgotten about. Even if you don't finish it. Try to keep any negative head chatter about it to a minimum, and enjoy the process.

CHAPTER SUMMARY:

- Get in the habit of taking a project from start to finish.
- If you are unhappy with a product, get feedback from someone ahead of you so you can learn how to do it better next time.
- Constraints can be the creative's biggest blessing.

QUESTIONS TO PONDER:

1) What stops me from completing a project?
2) What is one step I can take today to move toward the finish line in a stalled project?

NOTES:

CHAPTER 17

THE MOPEY PLACE

Creatives can get completely derailed in pity parties and with what I like to call 'the mopey place.' I call it this to separate it from legitimate depression. The mopey place feels the same as depression, but it is much more akin to a pity party. In my students, this most often manifests in their lessons when they feel guilty because they didn't work the past week at all. They come into the room and change the atmosphere because they feel horrible about themselves for not practicing. They come in guilty, depressed, and unhappy. This kind of a start to a lesson is rough and makes it very difficult to have anything productive happen until we get some hope and positivity into that mind of theirs. This moment is different than someone coming in with legitimate pain or loss. What I am describing feels more like 'I quit' or 'I give up' or 'I can't learn.'

A student who lives in the mopey place will come in week after week and sit on my piano bench with a 'harumph' attitude, waiting for me to do something. They often feel unmovable and unteachable, and I am left with no choice but to spend their lesson time helping to shift their emotions back toward neutral before beginning to teach. It is impossible for someone to learn anything with their emotions in that guilty place. Picture trying to take a sloth on a leash for an exhilarating jog.

Often the pity parties I see are tied directly to guilt and a lack of self-discipline. It is essential that creatives learn to overcome the tendency to embrace guilt and self-shaming. If they don't, they will usually quit lessons feeling quite bitter about things and maybe even bitter toward their teacher/mentor for not getting them to where they want to be in their craft. It's not only the lack of practicing that needs addressing, it's also the fact that they choose to wallow in a bath of self-loathing for even longer than they didn't practice. If this is you reading this and you are resonating with this, I want you to know that you have a place, there is hope, and there is always time to grow. If this is you, the first step is acknowledgement. It isn't your teacher's fault you aren't growing. **Your growth is your responsibility,** and if you want to grow, then grow! There's a good word right there—grow.

You might even be feeling guilty just reading this. Guilt is a valuable emotion sometimes, but I would say in regards to time spent working on your craft, **guilt is completely irrelevant** and a stumbling block to young artists. If you missed two days of creative time and then feel horrible about it, does that change your current situation? No, the situation is the same. Does it help your current mood? NO. Guilt makes you feel worse about yourself. Does it give you the energy and motivation to create today? For sure not. Guilt makes you want to escape and hide away in a lethargic state. What guilt does is give you a big case of the mopes. This is a place you really want to avoid as an artist.

Generally, when I was in the middle of a good self-involved wallow, all I wanted to do was eat fried cheesy food and watch television all day under a blanket. Powerful creatives who get to exciting places have learned to avoid this area because it is so unproductive. I am not saying that life and/or art needs to be cheerful and rosebuds all the time either. Life is full of joy and pain, peace and sorrow. It is almost impossible to go through life without experiencing pain or sorrow, but there is a big difference between genuine sadness and mope, between real pain and an artistic pity party meant to glorify suffering. You can perform, paint, write about very painful things without being in a wallowing session. Take the blues for instance; in this genre of music, the lyrics are about things that are painful, have gone wrong, or are unjust. Blues songs are almost never sung from a place of self-pity. I have yet to hear one anyways. Generally, they are sung from a 'Man, I been through hard times, y'all. Do you feel me?' place and not the 'I've given up' place. Take B.B. King's *Why I Sing the Blues* for example. It is a song about racism, the ghettos, and the many unjust hardships he experienced. But it is also a song that has such a great groove to it, and B.B.'s spirit isn't broken when he sings it. Bruised, but not broken. The little catchphrase I throw at the students who tip easily into the pity parties is 'say nope to the mope.' Lol. It's catchy and stays in their heads, but feel free to come up with a more dignified sounding catchphrase if you wish.

Also, be aware of when you are most vulnerable to a case of the mopes. Often when I am physically tired, I am more susceptible to having a depressed, self-involved day. In those moments, what you put into your ears, media-wise, and into your body, food-wise, will often determine which way the rest of the day goes (which we will talk about in the next chapter). If you are tired or going through legitimate pain, give yourself the grace to rest, sleep, and process.

This next student and I have been on quite the journey together. At the beginning of our time together, she would dive into a good self-shaming session easily, and then defend herself to me about how it was part of the artistic journey to wallow and suffer as a creative. She also wrote several songs that would take the listener so low and leave them there at the end of the song. I remember one song in particular, but I'll let her tell you about it.

Ashley's Story:

"In my first year of lessons with Heidi, I was in a really dark and insecure place. My mind was poisoned by my own self-loathing, and I thought I would never stop hating myself. I wrote a song about the voice in my head that was my biggest enemy, that rained on every single one of my parades, the reflection that only judged and insulted. I sang this song for Heidi one day thinking she would appreciate how real the song was. She did not. She told me that it was too defeated and unforgiving. She recommended that I leave the listener with some hope, some message that it would work out, that it wouldn't be like this forever. I was immediately opposed. I argued that life isn't a fairy tale and doesn't always have a happy ending and that I didn't want to delude my listener into thinking that was the proper expectation. I told her truth sometimes meant embracing sadness, and I was sad. Heidi responded that nothing lasts forever, so I wouldn't be lying if I wrote an uplifting ending. Instead, my listener would maybe find hope that things will work out for them.

"It took me some time, but I forced myself to write a happier ending to the song. I wrote about loving myself, about standing up to that voice in my head, and about not being a slave to her anymore. I was still sad, but the words of my song actually made me feel better. And gradually, I was happier. I didn't let the negative voice in my head rule my actions, I became kinder to myself, and eventually, miraculously, I was okay. Heidi was right. The pain was only temporary, and had I left the song as it was, it would have told every listener that their pain and mine was permanent. The song means so much more to me now because of the journey I had to take with it and with myself. Here are the lyrics with the changed ending.

"Chained to You"

Chorus 1:

She tells me I'm worthless and terrible

I'm broken, unbearable

I'm selfish, ungrateful

And I have too much that I don't deserve

I'm conceited and so needy

I can try all I want, but I'll never succeed

In the silly things I want most in this world

I try to talk her down

But she laughs as she pulls my strings

I scream just as loud

But all I hear is my own voice echoing

Final Chorus:

I tell her

I'm not worthless or terrible

Maybe broken, but repairable

Maybe selfish, but I'm not perfect, sometimes I'll make mistakes

I'll deserve it, I'll be worth it

I'm not there yet, but I'll work for it

I'll be patient and kind, and I'll give more than I take

I'll love way too much, I'll be strong, and I'll try to be brave

I'll be ready for your scars

I'll be ready for your wounds

I'll stand tall and proud

And one day, I won't be chained to you

Learning to show grace to ourselves for our imperfections is one of the essential skills of the artistic journey. We are all learning, growing, changing, and it's okay to be in process. The problem is when a creative isn't growing, evolving, or bettering themselves. And in all seriousness, I really encourage you to not run into sorrow or a case of the mopes with open arms. Very little of value is accomplished at a pity party and there is already enough sorrow in the world to process and deal with. The mopey place can have many different roots that cause it to come up; comparison to someone better than you who you think you'll never live up to, rejection, disappointment etc. Whatever the cause of the mope, the key is to learn not to run into it willingly.

MINDFUL MEDITATION:

"My identity is not found in my accomplishments. I process my emotions, and I choose joy. I learn from all that happens, to me and/or because of me, and I move forward. I breathe deeply and embrace life. I see my way forward and reclaim my purpose with joy."

MOTIVATIONAL MOMENT:

Go spend thirty minutes on a project of your choosing.

CHAPTER SUMMARY:

- With regard to your craft, guilt is irrelevant.
- Avoid running into depression with open arms.
- There is a difference between genuine sorrow and a pity party.
- Say nope to the mope.

QUESTIONS TO PONDER:

1) Do I throw a pity party when I feel guilty or disappointed?
2) Do I have the ability to show myself grace when I am tired?
3) Do I allow real pain to express itself in a healthy way so I can move past it, or do I trap it inside me and keep it with me?

NOTES:

CHAPTER 18

YOU BECOME WHAT YOU LISTEN TO

Music and media have the ability to change your internal emotional atmosphere and energy without your permission. Have you thought about that? That is something that I think about every day. Let's do an example. If you listen to Adele's "Hello" on repeat and try to maintain an inner state of joy and excitement . . . it is extremely difficult! You are fighting the darker atmosphere of the song for a full six minutes and seven seconds. On a happy day, I can maintain my contented inner atmosphere when listening to a beautiful song like "Hello" and revel in its artistic beauty . . . but when I am tired and feeling a little beaten down, I choose my music and media so carefully, like a supreme guardian at the gates of my eyes and ears. Whatever goes into my ears or eyes needs to be something that can bring me up or relax me, not something that takes me lower. I used to tell students, "You are what you listen to," because I would see so many emotional teenagers struggling with depression and self-harm. When I would take a look at what was on their playlist, it was music that helped feed into that depressive state, not learn to overcome it. Some of you would say that music that expresses how you are feeling helps you push through something because you identify with the writer. I would say, okay, but if you are low, does the music cause you to stay low for an extended period of time or allow you to express yourself and neutralize?

Legitimate pain has a right to express itself in your body, and it is best to deal with it, express it, and get it processed in a healthy way. What I won't tolerate for myself, however, on a day when I am physically exhausted but content with my life, is to have a song that I listen to take my emotions into depression and leave them there so that I spend the day fighting off the depression that wasn't mine to begin with. I am actually battling the songwriter's depression. On the occasion that I fall into this trap, I feel annoyed with myself for allowing myself to be shifted down emotionally by someone else's pain. I always pay attention to how music makes me feel and weigh carefully whether I will engage with it based on the state of mood I'm in that day.

Only you will know how a song affects you and whether it benefits you or not. When I listen to heavy metal, I feel powerful, intense, angry, and even a little rebellious, but I have a former student who listens to metal, and it calms her down. We are all different. I have had only three students in ten years whose emotions were not influenced by media at all. They could listen to the darkest of suicidal songs and be in their logical brains about that song, whereas I, as a sensitive feeler, was reeling and trying to safeguard myself in the lesson from the doom I felt listening to it. We are all different. The point I am trying to get across to you is to pay attention to how you feel and what you let inside your eye and ear gates. How is it affecting you? How is it affecting your day? Is it bringing you up or down? I will say it again: **music and media can change your emotions without your permission.** How do **you** want your emotions changed today? Pick your media accordingly.

Another thing to keep in mind is that you will be influenced by the people you follow on social media as well as the people you surround yourself with. If you are a highly motivated creative, then this doesn't matter so much, but if everyone you follow on social media is complaining about the government, politics, life, and the pandemic, then what is going in my eye gate is usually a downward influence on my day. I have chosen to stay friends with really negative people on social media, but I usually unfollow them so that I am not getting barraged by all their angry thoughts at the start of my day. I also generally don't surround myself with people like that in person. I am an outgoing introvert who gives a lot of who I am to my students. In the evenings, I am unwilling to spend my energy dealing with negative, angry people. That may sound selfish, but for me it is necessary so I am not left dry with nothing for myself or nothing to give away to my students. Picture some epic fantasy scene like Gandalf fighting the Balrog in *The Lord of the Rings*. You are the guardian of your eye and ear gates, and you choose what you let get past them.

MINDFUL MEDITATION:

> "I guard my heart with what brings life. I feed my soul things that bring purpose to it. My choices elevate my body, soul, mind, and spirit. I take responsibility for my choices. I embrace abundant life."

CHAPTER SUMMARY:

- Music and media can change your emotions without your permission.
- Become a guardian over your eye and ear gates.
- Choose what media you do or don't consume based on your emotional and physical equilibrium that day.
- The people I surround myself with matter.

QUESTIONS TO PONDER:

1) How much of an influence does media and music hold over my day?

2) Am I a good guardian over my eye and ear gates?

3) Are there toxic things or people in my life that I can reduce the influence of?

NOTES:

CHAPTER 19
ARROGANCE AND SELF-SUFFICIENCY

On the flip side of fear is arrogance or pride. There is good pride, in which you are satisfied and content with your accomplishments, but there is also arrogant pride that makes a student unteachable. I have had only a few students like this, as they don't usually want to stay very long. Someone like this believes they know more than everyone around them and are usually in music lessons to show me, their teacher, how much more they know and to impress me with their brilliance and self-sufficiency. They are very difficult to mould or shape because they already have their set path and opinions. These people already have the style of songs they like to sing or dance to and are unwilling to open their minds to any new ideas.

If this is you, I think it is fabulous that you have such a well-developed sense of identity, and I pray it works out well for you. I wish you success, but I also think this trait might shoot you in the foot someday. First of all, arrogance is really smelly to be around. If someone thinks they know it all and are better than everyone else, they will give off a certain vibe to those around them. Very few people will want to work with them because of that arrogance. The arts are so much about community that if one person makes it a 'them show,' they might get hired in a company for a year, but then lose their spot. I am not saying this to put fear in you, I am just letting you know that what you bring to a room, the presence you bring with you, your energy, your vibe, matters! Do you light up a room when you walk in or do you bring it down?

A concept that I want to give you is **try to learn something from anyone and everyone you come across in your field.** Be a permanent student, a sponge, always willing to soak up something new and improve yourself. If you think you have it all learned and are good, that's usually a sign that you haven't even begun your journey yet. Some of my students are in bands in churches and when they don't understand something in a rehearsal, they keep silent because they don't want to look foolish in front of their friends. Then they privately ask me about the things they didn't understand in a lesson. In these instances, my students' unwillingness to look weak in front of their peers is a hindrance to their team that is rehearsing that evening. By hiding their mistakes, instead of asking questions and sorting it out with their team, they are actually affecting the progress of the group that evening. I strongly encourage those students to ask their peers questions when they are confused in a rehearsal. If your peer can do something that you cannot and is willing to help you for free (when you usually have to pay for one-on-one instruction) then why not accept it from them?

I challenge you to begin looking around at others in your field of interest for anything they carry that you are missing and ask them for help!

Also, on the flip side, be willing to give away something you have in return for free. Try to learn something from everyone you meet. It's not always possible, I realize, but be open to it. I am reminded of a moment a long time ago when I was at a small country church service and heard an elderly couple get up to sing a duet. And well, God bless them, but it didn't sound good to my ears. The wife had a wobbly crow-like voice, and it was one of the funniest sounds to my ears. My first instinct was to approach their gift with superiority and giggle at their offering. But a small voice inside me said, "Heidi, stop that and listen." I turned off my music ears and started listening with my heart to what this beautiful lady was trying to give away. At the end of the song, I was in tears because of the way she had sung from her heart. I was also seriously humbled from my ugly and superior attitude. I am not saying she was the best singer on the planet, but if you have an attitude inside you that says, 'What can I learn from them? What are they trying to communicate?' you will often be blessed with something. Maybe it's even what 'not' to do. This attitude will get you far. It's also an attractive attitude that makes people want to be around you. Learn how to become teachable. Learn how to stay teachable.

Another interview I recommend watching is a Carol Burnett interview from *The Dick Cavett Show*. The comedy legend gets asked if there are kinds of people she won't work with again and she lists off some of the ridiculous behaviour she's encountered over the years of being in 'the biz.' She reminds us that there should be an element of play in our work. Take a look for it later and make sure you aren't giving off any of the qualities from that list! The point I am trying to make is that attitude matters.[13]

Something I bring up with all my students who want a future career in the arts is the concept of 'Character before Gifting,' which I initially heard in church services, but don't let that keep you away from something really good because it applies to this kind of thing as well. Let me explain. This phrase means that who you are is more important than what you do. Take a second to think about that. Who you are as a person is more important than what you do. Gulp. That's sometimes so hard to compute for me.

The picture I give my students here is one of a bench or a small table. The legs holding up the bench represent your character. Your character is who you are, what you believe in, your views, what you stand for, what you won't stand for, how you treat people, your mental health practices and internal work toward self-betterment, etc. The legs represent all the parts of you that can't be seen in your product. The top of the bench is your gift—your dance, your photography, your poetry, your comedy, etc. Just as the legs support the bench and not the other way around, your character is what supports your gifting. Take a moment to let that image and thought sink in. Your character is what supports your gifting's success. The more successful you become, the more weight is put onto that table. If you only dabble in the arts, there is probably not a lot of weight being placed onto you and your gift. But if you are lucky enough to become super successful and make a career out of your gift, weight and pressure are put on by managers, agents, producers, fans, social media, etc. Picture heavy boulders being placed onto the table. What happens if those legs are wobbly and the screws are not tight? If your character isn't strong enough to support your gift, it will buckle. How many young singers and actors have we seen get famous before they could become secure in their own identity? What happens? Usually a public mess. I'm not going to call them out by name, but I could easily name ten off the top of my head. It is so much messier to try to figure out who you are and get yourself sorted out once you are in the spotlight with all eyes on you. Wouldn't you rather do the internal work in private before you ever get any recognition? Some of those young artists you are probably thinking about were lucky and were able to rebuild themselves, whereas others like Amy Winehouse are no longer with us. Taylor Swift is someone whom I respect in that way. As far as I can tell, she has not changed who she is because of the pressures of fame. She continues to pave her own way, has a trusted group of people surrounding her, and has never had to sacrifice huge amounts of authenticity or what she believes in for the sake of success.

> *"Be a positive, happy person, and treat everyone well. People really pick up on that. Work for free, it doesn't matter. I know you are not a cleaning person, that's not your job, but clean up after people, go get coffee, be as humble as you can, so people will allow you to be in the big rooms with them."*
>
> **Sanaa Kelley – Three-time Emmy Nominated Foley Artist**

I'll say it again: **Character before gifting. Who you are matters more than what you do.**

MINDFUL MEDITATION:

"I am not defined by success or failure. I recognize all of life that contributes to who I am and what I express with gratitude. My artistic expression comes from within. I listen to my heart and understand. I am not alone. I respect others. I choose to give and receive with a grateful heart."

CHAPTER SUMMARY:

- You bring an atmosphere with you when you enter a room.
- Table analogy—it is your character that supports your gifting.
- Stay teachable and learn from anyone you can.

QUESTIONS TO PONDER:

1) Will I say yes to anything to get to the top?
2) Am I on the inward journey as well as the upward journey? (Meaning, do I regularly practice self-betterment?)
3) Do I feel superior to those around me? If so, why?
4) How do/will I treat my assistants, my creative team?
5) Do I show up on time and prepared?

NOTES:

_____
_____
_____
_____
_____
_____
_____

CHAPTER 20
THE ARTISTIC ORPHAN MINDSET

Something that looks similar to arrogance but has a different root system is what I like to call the 'artistic orphan' mindset. This is such a good concept, one that I heard talked about in church environments, and I loved it so much that I modified it to be about the art world. I am by no means an expert on what it is to be an orphan, but we often hear stories from adults who grew up in the welfare system and how difficult it was. In the recent past, children in this system had all their belongings in one black garbage bag that travelled with them from foster home to foster home. Children who grow up in this very difficult system or within an actual orphanage often have to fight for things that they want because nothing is easy or handed to them. If there is a slice of pie and another child at the home takes a piece, there is one less piece left for them. So in a sense, that other child is taking their piece of the pie away from them.

What I have labelled in my studio as an 'artistic orphan' is someone that is fairly easy for me to recognize. Let me describe them for you. An 'artistic orphan' views success as something that is limited, like the pieces of pie. There is a limited amount of success out there, and if another performer gets some of it, that means they took my share away from me. Now there is less success out there, and I might not make it because that performer took it from me.

Artistic orphans view their peers as competition and are unable to celebrate their successes or form strong connections with their peers because they see them as a threat. They cannot promote anyone else's work because they want that promotion for themselves. They also network in a very specific way. The ones I have met, after shaking my hand and congratulating me on my performance, begin asking me about all the things I do musically. In moments like these, it feels like they are scanning me like a Borg Cube (there's the inner *Star Trek* nerd) to see if there are any parts they can extract for themselves to further their career. Then, if they have scanned me and realize I am of no use to them, they drop me, and then move on. I have unfortunately experienced this multiple times at open mic nights with local artists I had looked up to.

> *"If you want to go fast, go alone. If you want to go far, go together."*
>
> ### *Proverb*

Let me tell you something. There is enough success for everyone, as long as you are being your authentic self and continuing to work hard on yourself and your craft. Pie for everyone. Pie. For. Everyone. If this is you, stop for a second, and let this sink in: **no one else's success is a threat to your own.** If you claw your way to the top by stepping on and over people, what does that say about your character or who you have become? Please, do not be that way. Be kind to one another, as Ellen would say. There is a place in this industry that belongs just to you. You don't have to fight for it, it's yours already. Live right now like it's yours.

> *"I have something for you, kids. One piece of knowledge. Do not forget this. All the next leaders, when we are all gone and done with the business. They're right next to you right now. Make those connections. Everybody you're going to meet in the future is right beside you. Whether they're a dancer, actor, graphic designer, coder. They're right next to you. Get to know who's next to you. Get to know the people in your neighbourhood. That's one of the things I can give you to help you get successful in any part of your life you want to go in, not just entertainment."*
>
> **Jack Mills (jackmillsshow) – Producer, Emcee**

> *"Create as many connections and work with as many people as possible at the ground level because those people do move up and then take you with them."*
>
> **Ariel Marx – Film Score Composer**

If you believe that success is limited, aside from beginning to change your belief system, I am going to challenge you to start cheerleading some of your peers, people who are at the same point in their journey as you or maybe some who are even slightly ahead of where you wish you were. Share some of their photographs, poems, songs, and comment positively on their social media account. Become their champion! It might hurt a bit at first because you are breaking off a deeply entrenched mindset that has been there awhile, but this is one that is really worth getting rid of. Push through that and don't stop your cheerleading until you actually have genuine happiness in your heart for them. That will be how you will know you've won that battle—if you can celebrate others' successes. If they get there before you . . . great! You will get there too if you don't give up. Remember, **if you don't quit, you win.**

MINDFUL MEDITATION:

"I have all that I require to move forward. I ask and receive what is required for my present project. My past does not define me. I have abundance. All things are possible. I step into the fullness of my destiny, fully equipped. I am empowered."

CHAPTER SUMMARY:

- We are not in competition with each other.
- Learn to celebrate your peers' successes.
- There is enough success for everyone. Success isn't limited.

QUESTIONS TO PONDER:

1) Can I celebrate other people?
2) What are my beliefs surrounding success?
3) Do I compete with others or work with others?
4) Am I a lone wolf?
5) What is one thing I can do to network in a healthy way with some of my peers?

NOTES:

CHAPTER 21
CREATIVITY

We've talked a lot about things that hinder creativity, but for this chapter, I interviewed professional creatives in various fields about how they access creativity. What does it feel like when one is in creative flow? I will give you my personal creative process first.

One of the main things I would describe creativity as being like is a river. It flows. Once I step into it, if I stay there, it carries me through most of my project. When I am in the first moments of a new creative idea, I feel child-like excitement, giddiness, and passion. Those moments are my most favourite times. For me, there is a moment of spontaneity when an idea feels like it drops into my head. Then I take a moment and think it through. Can I roll with this idea? Is it feasible? As I process a good idea, I usually get more excited until I am convinced I can move forward with it. Then comes the less-fun follow-through. Usually, my excitement is enough to get me halfway through the follow-through, and then self-discipline takes me the rest of the way.

Emily Solstice Tait – Dancer

"I access creativity by connecting with other people. Their music, their images, their movies, their stories, their conversations, their problems, their dreams, their families, their disasters, their desires. Knowing that the art itself can be like a conversation or just a shared moment."

Victoria Patterson – Dancer, Dance Instructor

"Creativity feels like I can speak in different ways. I can put normal life aside. I'm inside this problem, in a free world that feels almost like a euphoric mental cocoon. It feels like a very safe clear bubble and, even though the world is happening around me, I can do whatever I want inside that bubble and the possibilities are endless."

I love this moment in the middle of a Paul Williams interview with *The Tennessean* . . .

> *"If you have a creative thought, and you have somebody to believe in what you're doing, and you have the element of faith involved, you can do anything. It all begins with some amazing creative source that we're just fortunate enough to tap into."*
>
> ***Paul Williams – Songwriter, Film Composer, Singer, Actor, Grammy Award Winner, President of the American Society of Composers, Authors, and Publishers***[14]

Maggie Regimbal – Author, Theatre Actor

"A lot of getting creative, for me, stems from drawing upon the other arts. I listen to music, especially instrumental music, read a book, look at visual art, or even play video games. Sometimes when I'm watching a television episode, it sparks the thought, *Oh, that would be such a cool idea if I could put this twist on it,* or when an episode or novel ends on a cliffhanger, it gets me thinking about what could come afterward and the possibilities. I really also like looking at art. Sometimes I will go on Pinterest and look at pictures of people and imagine a character and storyline for them. Music is really important to me. If I hear folk music, it often evokes fantasy images versus rock music, which would help evoke an action sequence. Sometimes when I am writing a sad scene, I like to listen to things that make me cry and that move me on an emotional level. I love listening to music for creating. When I am creative, I feel inspired, excited, peaceful, and very childlike.

"Really good ideas surprisingly often happen late at night for me. Sometimes they just come to me, but then I have to conjure up a plan and a way to make it work in my story. For example, using a character with magic might pop into my head suddenly, but then I would need to create a whole system so that magic makes sense to everyone and to the story. I have to give form to the idea. So there's an element of spontaneity to a good idea, but there is also an element of responsibility on my part to make it work.

"I get writer's block a lot. Especially when I look at my piece of work and start thinking, *it could be more,* or *it's not going to end up being that great anyway*. The biggest issue for me as a writer is often balancing dialogue, description, and plot. The fear of making the wrong decision is what often stalls me from moving forward in a book. Should I add a description paragraph here, or put more dialogue, or have an action sequence happen? When I'm not sure where I'm headed, these kinds of moments can really hinder. Usually, I'm worried that making the wrong choice will negatively affect my story later on or whether the readers will even like that choice.

"I am currently working on the second book of a trilogy and am stalling on penning a scene because I don't know if a character would react the way I am writing them. In order to move forwards, I have to stop, look back at my previous work in detail, and study the consistency of that character to get my answers.

"Sometimes to keep moving through a stuck moment, I will put brackets in with what I want to happen inside them. I put the problem area in brackets, continue on with my story, and then come back later to address the brackets. If it's a dialogue problem, I will probably have to talk through it with someone else and find out how they would react to a certain situation. For action sequences, sometimes I'll look up movie clips to watch how characters move in a fight scene and pull inspiration from that. Or I'll read someone else's action sequence in a book and see how they described something, like a punch. You don't want to spend five paragraphs on two thrown punches. You need to have your characters think thoughts or say something. Also giving myself a little bit of a break and then coming back to it helps me. Or getting back into feeling creative, by listening to music or watching some other media. Sometimes even venting my stress about a project to a trusted friend or family member will help me process and move forward. Even playing video games helps my mind to relax so that it can return to its creative state."

Glenn Radley – Singer-Songwriter, Multi-Instrumentalist @gladly

"In terms of process, the word 'process' itself is super important. I think as creative people, we have to acknowledge the fact that the muscle we are trying to strengthen creatively is the muscle of process. The way that we do that is by constantly creating. So personally, **any moment at any time is a good moment to come up with an idea.** As well as trying to generate content, you are also in the business of digesting content and making it a part of you, so finding influences that resonate with you is going to be huge. Then diving as deep as you can with that artist. **Always be creating.**"

JoAnn McFatter – Singer-Songwriter, Recording Artist

"Whatever you choose to do, however you choose to express, do it with all of your heart! That is what moves people. Your passion, your heart energy will come through. For a singer, the frequency of your voice holds all that is going on in your heart. There are even scientific studies referencing this. Your voice can be recorded, and they can tell what is going on inside you by reading the frequencies in your voice.

"In respect to that, singing or painting (or whatever your creative expression is) from your head will not move people the way engaging from your heart will. People know and feel the difference, even though they may not be able to explain it. They can feel your intention. There is a lot of research around this topic. The HeartMath Institute is a strong resource for this if you want to learn more. *Psychology Today* states, 'The upside is plentiful as to why we should increase our heart's harmony. With an electrical component about 60 times greater and an electromagnetic energy field 5000 times greater than the brain's, the heart has a significant influence on the body down to the cellular level. The brain's rhythms along with the respiratory and blood pressure rhythms entrain with the heart's rhythm. This is the optimal state for human functioning.[15]'

"My point is that releasing from your heart will move people and have a more lasting impact than from your head."

Ray Hughes – Master Level Creative

"Creativity to me feels like a 'what if' that won't go away until it becomes a 'what is.' One of the most liberating things a creative person will ever learn is the difference between a thought, an idea, and a dream. It will save you a lot of wear and tear on your heart if you can balance those three. A thought can come in a moment and never be remembered. We as creatives are always watching for the thought. We are always awake, always alert, always aware. It's a part of our process. An idea comes, and it stays long enough to create an inner conversation. Then a dream turns that conversation into something that shapes our destiny on some level.

"The way it works for me is I look at tree standing in front of my house and say, 'What a beautiful tree.' There's a thought. I might take one of those fallen limbs and make a knife handle out of it. There's an idea. Now I am going to build a company that makes the most beautiful knives that have ever been made and those knives will become keepsakes that pass from fathers to sons for generations. There's a dream. How we walk through that process is what determines how well we do with it—being able to discern which one is which and which one we value enough to never let it go. I say all three. If you put a month into it, on its own it turns from a thought to a dream.

"I'd also say we have to come to a place to give ourself permission to create, and then unapologetically just go ahead and drink from the chalice of our own imagination. We've refused to honour imagination. We've been taught as kids, 'Oh, that's just your imagination,' as if it were something wrong. In fact, I actually think one of the greater gifts we've been given is our imagination. If we can become a true imaginator, we will create from the place of what we see, what we hear, sense, and feel. We need a return to wonder, beauty, and imagination wrapped up in integrity. That's what makes a good combination for originality.

"Also ask the question, 'what is the truth in this that has become so real to me that it has made my life more beautiful?' and fit that into your art because whatever goes into your art has to go to your heart first. Otherwise, there's no originality to it whatsoever, you become an imitator and eventually, an imposter mechanically producing things."

MINDFUL MOMENT:

"I access my creativity from within and express freely. I trust my instinct and inspiration. I am an original voice, not an echo of another's expression. I love who I am and take joy in expressing myself fully. I am free to be me. My imagination thrives. I am able to express freely."

CHAPTER SUMMARY:

- Always be creating.
- Imagination is to be cherished.
- Use other media to inspire creative thought.
- Creativity can also be accessed through other people.
- Creativity should come from the heart.

QUESTIONS TO PONDER:

1) What does creativity feel like to me?
2) Is my art an honest reflection of what's in my heart?
3) Am I able to access creativity easily?

NOTES:

_____
_____
_____
_____
_____
_____
_____

CHAPTER 22
PROBLEMS CREATING

"What blocks creativity for me usually centres around worries: financial, self-worth, impossible timelines, and pandemic pivoting."

Emily Solstice Tait – Dancer

Hitting a creative block. We all do it. I don't know a creative who has never been stuck at least once. I see this often in my students when they are songwriting. They will write something, and then quickly erase it because they suddenly don't think it's any good. Everything they attempt to create gets torn down by their inner critic and the negative voices they hear in their head. If this pattern of creating and erasing goes on for too long, what ends up happening is that the student gives up and says, "I can't write songs," which then is a statement that becomes a belief. I have so many things to say about this kind of pattern. One of the first things is to tackle the lie-based thinking revolving around the block, which in this instance is things like, 'My songs are terrible, people won't like my songs, I can never finish a song, I am terrible at rhyming,' etc. Change your words. Change those beliefs! It's really gritty work, but it matters.

Something that helps my students overcome this problem is this really helpful concept that I made up for them: **creator vs critic.** Let me explain. Imagine inside of us are two separate parts when it comes to creating—creator and critic. Both are important. Both have a place and have value. The creator is responsible for the spark, the ideas, the flow. The critic, also important, will help carry you to the completion of your project and gauge whether or not things are working well. The trouble is when you try to create something and have both the creative and critic activated inside you at the same time. This almost always leads to the frustrating cycle of beginning something, and then walking away.

Learn to keep your inner critic turned completely off while you create. Creating should feel easy, childlike, and fun. Like fingerpainting. No negative thoughts, no doubts, just exploration of whatever you are trying to create. Once you are in the river, stay in the river until you have exhausted all ideas. This is so important because once you step out of the river during the creative process, it is really hard to get back in the same emotional or creative space the next day and continue with what you were feeling the day before. Often times this is where a large roadblock lives with one of my songwriters because they can't seem to get back 'in' the song to finish it. It is much easier if you never leave in the first place until you have everything you need. The best thing I can say to someone struggling to get back into a project is to either shake off the pressure and try to get your emotions back to where they were when you started and see if you can finish it yourself, or bring someone else into the project to get help taking it to the finish line. It is really hard in that 'stuck headspace' to finish a project by yourself. It's not failure, it's wisdom to get another brain in there to help you navigate past that block.

When your project is rough but complete, then is the time for the inner critic to come out. The inner critic can take a look at what's been made and ask, "What do I like? What needs editing and changing?" And then you can begin polishing up and editing your project until you are satisfied with it. If you are still unsure, get another set of eyes on it. Send it to some peers in your field. Ask your mentor what they think. Take a risk!

A tool I use (and hear others say often helps when creating) is to have some kind of music going on in the background to affect my mood. I usually prefer instrumental because I am writing my own lyrics, and I also like the music to match the feeling of what I am trying to express in my art. This also helps my brain not panic if I don't have an idea right away. Fear actually stops creativity. Full stop. Did you know that when you are afraid, the pathway to your prefrontal cortex actually shuts down? The prefrontal cortex is the part of your brain where you do all of your adult thinking. I think it is some kind of preprogrammed fight or flight instinct that is in our DNA. All that to say, it is really important to stay relaxed when you create and not overthink anything. Use whatever tools you have at your disposal to not panic or slip into fear.

> *"In a season where I feel less inspired, I go on walks, read books, go to the library, or the art museum. A lot of my creativity comes in quiet and aloneness. But I also enjoy absorbing other people's stuff, so I might go to the library or meet with a friend for coffee and pull from them. I don't have a lot of dry seasons just because I paint, write, and draw. If painting isn't going great, I can switch to drawing, or if drawing isn't going great, I can switch to writing. For my own self, I've needed to enjoy what I'm doing as much as pursuing what I'm doing. I've needed to enjoy doodling and doing my artwork as much as I've needed to pursue it to a point of excellence and a point of career."*
>
> ***Natasha Boone – Canadian Author and Artist***

The next two students who will be sharing with you both struggled with creativity. But it wasn't because of their critic, it was actually rooted in some toxic beliefs they were holding on to about their own value and the value of their words.

Ashlee's Story:

"I don't really know how I first started thinking this thought, but somehow the belief settled in me that what I had to say wasn't important enough to tell other people about. I started to believe the lie, and it led me to think that I shouldn't share what was really going on deep in my heart because it wouldn't resonate with anyone. So why would I bother sharing it? This can be said of many things in my life, but for me it came out specifically in writing songs. I just felt like I couldn't do it, so every time I heard of one of my friends writing a song, I told myself that I could never do it. Then one day I came to a lesson and told Heidi that I could never write a song, and she proceeded to tell me that I was going to write a song right then and there. She gave me forty-five minutes to finish it, and then she wanted to hear me sing it. I looked right at her and told her that I couldn't do it, but she left me alone to write in the church sanctuary. I ended up actually writing a pretty decent song and sang it publicly on the studio Instagram. Sometimes we feel like we are the only ones going through a specific thing and that we can't share it with anyone because they might judge us for what we are feeling or how we react to certain things. But we need to stop thinking those things because they aren't true, and our voice is VALID. It does matter. Don't ever let yourself think that it doesn't. For all you know, you expressing yourself could be the reason someone else also feels free to express themselves. You could give someone a new perspective on life. You could give them hope. This is why we need to realize that we all have a message to share."

Courtney's Story:

"For a long time, I thought my voice didn't matter. I thought no one wanted to hear my voice, hear what I played, or hear the songs I wrote. I had spent so much of my life feeling invisible even in my own friend group, so I was sure no one would listen to my music. It's not easy to overcome, and I still stumble and get stuck sometimes. But I have to remind myself that I can't make music for others, it has to be for myself because

I love doing it, that even if no one hears my song or thinks it is good, I made it because I love it. **Even if one person likes my song, it's worth it.**

"I still have to remind myself that **I am not invisible**, that people hear me and see me—in my music and otherwise—that I'm only invisible because I tell myself that I am."

> *"I want to give you the idea that there is power in talking about things that scare you. Sometimes the things that feel the scariest to talk about, are the things that might have the most impact on someone else. You don't realize right away, but they could get something very powerful from it. So all these things that you might keep inside, getting them out, getting them on paper, getting them outside of yourself really help in the healing process. Also really just sharing your voice with the world from a place of authenticity is a good place to start. These places usually scare you at first, but once they're outside of yourself, they become less scary.*
>
> ***Bret Paddock – Songwriter, Arranger, and Music Producer***

Again, so much of what stops us in our tracks are these sneaky little beliefs we hold as truth when they are not. Even writing this book, I have personally come up against a ton of them. Truth: your art should come out of what you feel and know. **Create what you know and trust that it has value.**

This leads me to another very common creative derailing. Don't create something for the sole purpose of pleasing other people. I mean, we all hope people will like our work, but if we create only so that other people will like it, that will create pressure, and our inner critic will become highly bothersome and loud when we are trying to create. The inner critic will shout things like, "Will this person like this?" and, "I wonder what these people will think of me when they see this?" while you are trying to be childlike and create effortlessly.

I once had a student who had a very good life, was very well-off financially, and was a generally well-adjusted, happy human being. Funny thing was, she often wrote songs that were just gut-wrenching, and in fact, some of them were downright shocking in how dark they were thematically.

There was also a ton of incongruity in her writing, and her songs didn't have a good flow to them. I finally asked her about where these songs were coming from and how she was doing in her personal life. Maybe behind closed doors her life was falling apart and her parents were getting a divorce or something of the sort. She reassured me that everything was great and revealed to me that she felt stupid and immature in writing happy songs. She thought the public would only respect songs that had mature themes with a lot of drama and heartache in them.

That is kind of adorable actually. See the belief that hindered the journey? How many songs can you think of that are happy that are hits? Tons! But because she believed no one would take her seriously unless she was going through deep pain, she was creating songs with fictional drama that she had never experienced and didn't know how to express or write about appropriately. The resulting songs were disjointed, dark, shocking, and songs that she herself couldn't even emotionally connect with while performing them. I will say it again, create out of what is inside you without thinking about whether or not other people will enjoy what you are doing. **It is most important that YOU enjoy what you are doing.** You need to love it. You need to feel satisfaction in your art.

Adeina Dey – Winnipeg Singer-Songwriter, Studio alumni, Recording artist

"Creating is definitely a part of you being released. Wherever you are in life and whatever you might be going through emotionally, that gets released through your creativity. I find most of my inspiration for my songs comes from my real-life experiences or those of someone close to me.

"It's a lot of fun creating art. It's fun to create something that you can show people and be proud of. In really hard times, creating gave me an outlet to release my feelings because when you are singing them or performing them, you feel heard.

"I think there's a sense of peace that comes with creating. It is almost like writing in a diary and getting something off your chest. It's something that has to be—you're not okay unless you do it. It's true. Art is meant to be made. I think there's a certain passion that is awakened when you're able to be creative. It's so different than anything else in life. Maybe it's similar to bringing a child into the world, bringing something new into the world. Something new and something exciting. I am the most creative when I take a moment from my busy life and give myself the space to just be. I think of the last song I wrote. I was taking my makeup off, and it just came to me. I should have gone to bed, but I wrote a song. A lot of the things you create are just a bubbling over of your thoughts and emotions. It's an expression.

"Don't worry so much about what comes out when you first start because you can come up with a bunch of ideas. Don't worry about the first idea being bad; sometimes your first idea is bad, but sometimes your tenth idea is good. No one will create the same as you create, dance the same as you dance. Who you are is unique and has value. Not only that, I think that it is important to have that release. Being creative is a journey into self-discovery as well. It gives insight into so many things that are going on inside of you. There are so many songs I've written that I realized were actually about myself after they were finished. Not only that, but it's very interesting that my songs are sometimes about the present and also sometimes written for my future self. I'm often reminded in a tough moment of an older song that I wrote that pertains to the current moment and speaks to it. Your creation is a gift to yourself and to the people around you. I think art is timeless, and it will always speak to someone. Watch, I'll be reading this book years later, and my own words will be exactly what I need to hear someday."

I love what Adeina just said: "Your creation is a gift to yourself." That is the best way to think about it. If we think about who's going to like or dislike our art while we try to create, stress will grab ahold of us. Impressing is stressing. Oooh, I just made that up on the spot, but it works. Remember that: **Impressing is stressing.** The only thing we can control is creating truthfully and authentically with what's inside of us to the best of our abilities. That's it. That's all we can control, so it's good to let go of all the things we can't. Take a minute to picture yourself carrying the weight of other peoples' opinions and reviews. Using your imagination, just let it go. Picture all that heaviness falling to the ground, then take in some deep cleansing breaths for the meditation.

MINDFUL MEDITATION:

"I accept my emotions and thrive. I create freely. I tap into limitless inspiration. There is no ceiling to my imagination and inspiration. I choose to see. I enjoy life. I am vibrantly alive to all that is within and around me. I express with ease."

MOTIVATIONAL MOMENT:

Go and do your favourite indoor or outdoor activity that puts you in a creative mood for thirty minutes. If any ideas come to the surface, write them down.

CHAPTER SUMMARY:

- Creator and critic should not be active at the same time.
- Your voice matters and your experiences are worth sharing.
- Learn how you actively get into your creative place.
- Creating is a part of you being released.
- Impressing is stressing.

QUESTIONS TO PONDER:

1) Can I create easily?
2) What hinders my creative process?
3) What steps can I take to make my creating joyful, childlike, and easy?
4) Is my art a true reflection of myself and my beliefs or thoughts?

NOTES:

_____
_____
_____
_____
_____
_____
_____
_____

CHAPTER 23

KEEP DREAMING, LIVE IN REALITY

When we think about the dreams and visions we have for our futures, most of us usually feel excitement, contentment, or happiness. Dreams are an essential part of being an artist, and even being a human being. A lot of the time, they are the motivation that fuels our work and the destination that we strive and labour toward. Having said that, I have recently bumped into a couple scenarios where dreaming was actually the problem and the obstacle. Two students come to mind who will be sharing their struggles with this at the end of the chapter. The first is Jayson, who wants a career as a music producer and performer and who, as I am writing this paragraph, just finished his first year of music lessons with me. Within his first couple weeks in lessons, Jayson would ask me questions like, "Heidi, should I have this as my band name?" "Heidi, when I am on tour, should I go to these cities?" "Heidi, will my manager expect me to . . ." etc., etc. He was also spending quite a bit of his money on new gear as a brand-new musician. He would say, "Heidi, I am going to build the most top-notch recording studio right here in my backyard—it's going to be epic!" "Heidi, I am going to buy all these instruments so my music sounds better." All this time, he had not completed his second song and was not investing daily time into creating and producing. My answer to all these questions was a firm, "Jayson! Have you finished your second song yet?!" "Uh no. not yet," he would say with a sheepish grin. "Have you worked on creating something every day this week?" I would ask him. "Uh no, I was watching YouTube videos on how to build a recording studio in my backyard," he would admit. See the problem? If you have big dreams like Jayson does, then you need to actually commit to **doing the thing every day** that will accomplish your dreams. If you are a dancer, the most expensive pointe shoes are not a guarantee that you will be hired. If you are an artist, the nicest brushes and most expensive canvases are not magical guarantees people will notice your work. These things in themselves are not bad, and they are sometimes necessary as I mentioned in the previous chapter, but what really counts is your product! Thought to ponder: **stuff does not equal status.**

> *"I think that limitations can bring out a lot of creativity. So it's not about owning a lot of gear or having the best sample libraries. With the smallest of resources, you have to be really creative to make something that is good. I do a lot with very little."*
>
> *Herdís Stafánsdóttir – Professional Film Composer*

Are you writing poems? Are you choreographing new dances and learning new routines? Are you spending time sculpting? Do you know the ins and outs of your editing program? If you have big dreams but aren't actually moving, maybe get together with a mentor or manager and look at the steps you need to be taking daily to get there. Like Natasha Boone talked about earlier, sometimes accountability will keep you moving forward, having another person that you are responsible to. Dreaming is awesome, keep dreaming, but don't live your whole life in there. Dreams without feet to them are just that—dreams. Side note: Jayson spends a solid hour most days now creating and has two songs out on iTunes already!

Jayson's Story:

"Hello, everyone, my name is Jayson, and at the time of writing this piece, I will have been taking music lessons with Heidi for about nine months, and I knew absolutely nothing about music when I started. In those first few months, I would think of being famous, and I would live in that dream and not think about what I should be doing now so that I could actually get to where I wanted to go. I was thinking about how tours would work, and I was trying to buy all this expensive equipment that a music producer would need. However, Heidi made me realize what I needed to do was to put my boots on the ground, so to speak. I needed to actually start practicing, start doing, and not just look and watch other people do what I wanted and wished I could do. I would say it took around six months before this finally dawned on me. Nothing I bought or owned was going to make my personal skill of making music any better. I needed to create, and I needed to actually finish songs, even if they were awful.

"Coming to terms with that is something I am still working on today. I have finished some full tracks and am working on making more. The effort it takes to put in at least an hour each day dedicated to making music is a lot more than I thought it would be. Some mornings it really is hard to get up and try. It was frustrating for me at first to dig in and just run against the metaphorical wall of no ideas, feeling like I wasted hours every day, feeling like I did nothing that helped me make it out the other side. I still sometimes struggle with living in the future and in my dreams.

I do still have times where I want to just buy something new instead of learning the software that I have. But it's a process."

Another amazing student of mine who has plans to release albums and dominate the music world has parents who really wanted them to pursue education instead of the arts. My student defended their position to their parents for years while growing up, telling them they were going to become a world-famous singer and make so much money. Unfortunately, those big words came back and became an obstacle for my student.

This student had not released any singles or released one music video, even though they could, and had not begun production of any of their many really well-written original songs, even though they went to school for music production and had a wealth of creative ideas. BUT when I talked with them about their career, they were already planning their big music video and planning to spend $10,000 on it. They were convinced that after one music video, they would get signed by a label and everything for them would be set for life. Um. Really? No.

I spent an entire music lesson arguing with them. Literally. One exhausting hour. This to date is the only student I have ever fully shouted at. Because of their bold personality, it was necessary for me to get loud for that student to hear me. I couldn't figure out why they were stalling on making a single move, yet still planning their global domination as an artist. I spent an hour arguing about how you cannot save and work for a year and expect one $10,000 music video to get you signed and set for life. It is much better that you learn to do a music video or project for free first. I say this because as I stated earlier, every time you release something, you make a ton of mistakes, and that's how you learn to do it better. If you are going to put everything you have into one video . . . what do you do when it flops and nothing happens? Work for another year, then try again? Even with my arguing, I was getting nowhere with this student, who was equally feisty and arguing passionately and loudly about how their big plans were absolutely going to succeed. And while I love the determination, I prefer not to put all my apples into one unsteady, unreliable basket.

Patric Scott, a well-known singer-songwriter from Switzerland, said to my music studio students, "You never know what will happen. You can have a big major deal and work your hardest and nothing ends up working. Or you could be on the street and someone films you singing one song, and you end up with a huge hit. **There is not a key you can turn** and have the doors open for you."

After much arguing, we finally pieced together what the block was. Surprisingly enough to both of us, it was fear. They had said such big grandiose things to their parents about how big they were going be and how they would dominate the industry and become world famous that they were **afraid to start small.** The pressure of their own big talk actually crippled their ability to take a step, even a baby step, in the direction of their dreams. It was actually a relief to unearth the reason behind the block. This student has had their first single release now with an album plan and an EP on its heels. They are working toward these goals now with a producer from Toronto, and I absolutely cannot wait until I get to have their songs on my iPhone playlist. They are now moving between steps A and B instead of planning Z. Don't be afraid of starting small.

Once you can shine a light on something and expose it, you can begin to move past it. If you cannot figure out what the block is, how do you remove it? It's actually so helpful when you can put words to the block and give it a name. I can completely understand why they spoke that way to their parents as a young teen, but to avoid this self-sabotage, my advice would be: **When you talk to people about your career, never say anything that isn't true**. Tell people exactly where you're at.

I actually remember talking myself up at an open mic years ago when I was first meeting other musicians. I told people I was a music producer when in fact, I had just downloaded the recording program and barely knew how to use it. The problem with talking yourself up to people is that then you will have to live up to exactly what you said you were with them. It is best to introduce yourself precisely where you are at so that you can be authentically yourself. Then the anxiety and stress of living up to any fiction you had described is not there because you said who you were clearly in the first place. I am reminded of a *Friends* episode where one of the characters had written down that they could speak French on their resumé. The show plays out hilariously as they frantically try to learn the entire language in one night before their audition. These things never go well. **Don't flippe flunque.**[16]

MINDFUL MEDITATION:

"I accept where I am at and move forward. I embrace all experiences from small beginnings to fulfilling my dreams. I enjoy the complete journey and love the learning process. I love who I am and where I am right now. I move forward each day in my journey."

CHAPTER SUMMARY:

- Dreams need actions in order to become reality.
- Don't be afraid to start small and take your first step.
- Avoid talking yourself up higher than you are to other people.

QUESTIONS TO PONDER:

1) Is there anything internal stopping me from taking a step forward in my career?

2) What is the balance of time that I spend dreaming about my career versus actually doing the things that will get me a career?

NOTES:

_____
_____
_____
_____
_____
_____
_____

CHAPTER 24

IT'S TOO LATE FOR ME, IMPOSTER SYNDROME, AND A POTPOURRI OF SELF-DOUBT

"I was forty-three when I got a Ph.D. I was fifty-one when I started my dream job. I was fifty-four when I married the love of my life. I was fifty-five when I ran my first marathon. I was sixty-seven when I self-published my first book. I turn seventy next year, and I can't wait. If you're thinking it's just not happening fast enough for you, hey, maybe you're just a late bloomer like me."

Douglas Lumsden[17]

People like Douglas Lumsden are so inspirational to me because sometimes when you teach teenagers and you are forty, it's easy to believe that it's too late for your dreams. But I read that quote and think, *Wow, life's exciting, I wonder what's in store for me?* My student Cameron also had this mindset, which prevented him from even trying to see if maybe he had a good singing voice.

Cameron's Story:

"As a sixteen-year-old guy living out in the country with no prior music experience in any shape or form, the thought of ever doing anything musical at this point in my life seemed way out of reach. I had never practiced any instrument, never tried improving my voice. I didn't even really know what my own voice sounded like. I always had the dream of actually being up on a stage and singing in front of an audience, but as a kid, that thought was always pushed to the back of my mind. In recent years, though, I thought, *Oh, you're too old for it by now; you're way past your prime learning years, and you should have practiced when you were a kid.* I just didn't think that someone who hadn't had a single voice lesson, hadn't practiced improving their voice one bit in sixteen years could ever catch up to the others. I believed I had to already have had some sort of amazing talent at this point to be able to sing anywhere. Boy, was I wrong. It only took a big enough spark for me to decide that I would try out voice lessons for the first time and see how far I could take the singing. I started virtual lessons in October 2020, and I actually gave myself a chance to see what would happen if I tried. And in a mere seven months, I've already been accepted into a band. It's so incredibly wild to me how, really, the biggest thing holding me back was myself. I just had to have confidence in myself and put myself out there and allow myself to improve.

"**The perfect time to start practicing and improving is right now.** You will never know how good you can get unless you actually put the effort in. You don't have to be some sort of prodigy before stepping in either. I know that was a thought I had before starting to work on my voice, but that's really the whole point of taking lessons. Everybody who is good at something was right where you are at some point, right at the bottom. Put yourself out there just to see what happens. It only takes one spark for something massive to happen."

Then again, sometimes it's your location that feels like a limitation. Notice I say feels like, because as long as you have access to the internet, you have an online audience that you can perform to and build. Some of the teens I teach in smaller towns struggle with thoughts like, 'Nothing ever happens here, so nothing exciting will ever happen to me.' Reagan has been one of those who's felt that strongly. Here are his thoughts.

Reagan's Story:

"I come from a tiny little town in Manitoba. The thing with my town is that pretty much everyone within a twenty-kilometre radius of the place is either a farmer or works for a manufacturing company. This is all good, unless you are a teenage boy who wants to sing and start spending money on a music career. Then suddenly the expectations of the community come out, to put your nose to the grindstone and work your entire life, barely scraping by. If you don't do that, then you are considered lazy or unmasculine. What that turns into is a lack of a music scene and feeling like you will never be able to make something of yourself in the industry because there is literally nowhere to go with it. I've had to learn to put myself out there with my music, even though I'm sure that most people around me wish that I was doing something more 'productive' with my time. That thought is something I have had to keep pushing down. I need to keep working and trying to find—and make—my own opportunities."

The next story comes from one of my student teachers, who taught the younger ones in my studio for me for around five years. During these years, she was a part of my student band, the mastermind editor behind our studio music video, and my strong right arm. I cannot tell you how much I appreciate this human. Unlike the other students, she decided to write about her challenges in teaching music for me and her internal struggle rather than her own musical obstacles.

Ainsley's Story:

"For me, I think the most challenging thing I faced with music was teaching for Heidi. I had imposter syndrome through the roof because my faith in myself was so shaky (even though I didn't realize it at the time). Heidi and I had so many talks about how I could approach something with a student or what concepts to go over, but all our talks ended up in the same place—with Heidi saying, 'I trust you.'

"After a while, the repetition made me understand that a piece of my self-confidence was missing: I didn't trust **myself**. I didn't trust myself to be able to explain a concept to someone, even though I wrote it out and rehearsed it before a lesson. I didn't trust that I knew my lyrics, even when I prepared for hours and hours. I didn't trust that I could hit a note, even though I had many times before. I didn't trust myself, my abilities, or even my education because I felt in my heart that I didn't know what I was doing. This realization opened my eyes to the fact that I still had to work on myself, even though I thought I had 'conquered' my self-esteem issues already.

"So, I went back and reflected on some of Heidi's and my other talks, and I found something I had written down: 'Being a great artist requires a lot of hard work, but the most important work is on yourself—start with truly believing you have something in you worth sharing.'

"It's easy to let an idea into your head, but it's an entirely different thing to let it into your heart and truly believe it. In that moment, I realized that I didn't actually believe I had something to offer. I had found the blind spot in my internal work, and I wanted to change that.

"I physically wrote down things I was proud of myself for and would read it out loud, over and over. These were cold, hard facts that my brain would try to diminish or change, but I would repeat them anyway. After a while, they really started to sink in. My brain shifted from saying the words and immediately hearing 'no' in my head, to hearing that 'no' get quieter and quieter.

"I'm still not perfect. I still doubt myself all the time, but the difference is that now I can catch myself in those moments and remind myself of the truth. Now I'm able to (sometimes) let go and really trust that all my hard work will pay off—but I also realize that doing this kind of work on myself is an ongoing process as an artist. It's completely exhausting, but it's always worth it."

My next student, Marshal, is someone you would never guess struggles with second-guessing himself. Lol. His online personality is so bold, funny, and original, you'd never think that doubt would be his constant internal companion.

Marshal's Story:

"I don't really know where to begin with this. Self-doubt. Y'all know it. Some of y'all have it. Some of y'all are still probably struggling with it, as am I. It's something that affects us in our work, hobbies, and especially our art. It makes showing other people our art difficult. If you have a rough draft or a demo, showing it to someone else feels like you're physically taking a piece of yourself off and giving it to them. Personally, I have my own deep struggle with it. Something in me keeps telling me that my work isn't good, and I should just quit. No one's going to like it, and I'm going end up broke and on the street. Sometimes that voice keeps coming back and coming back, and I keep trying to push it away because it's not the truth. But it just **WON'T. SHUT. UP.** All of our little voices come from different places, and I can tell you where my voice comes from. As strange as it sounds, it comes from my YouTube channel, Marshal Does Stuff. The short of it is, I used to make one type of content, but I stopped at some point. Afterwards, I really started to tank in views. So, because of that, I really started to doubt . . . EVERYTHING. My YouTube content, my ability to make that content, and especially my music. A lot of it is comparing my music to other people's music. *Oh yeah, my music is okay, but it's not as good as this other guy's.* I kept doubting that my music was any good, and because of that, I made music a lot less frequently. The thing about self-doubt is that at some point it just becomes normal to you. You get used to it and it becomes comforting. Now, I'm not at the end of the journey of getting through my self-doubt, but I know what can help me is helping me. Firstly, having people in my life like Heidi who can bring the logic back in me and say that my work is great. Secondly, actually just telling yourself that you're worth it every day feels weird, but it is really effective. You really start to rely less on other people for affirmation. Thirdly, therapy is just good for ANY mental issue you have. Especially if you're younger and you can deal with those problems early. So yeah. That's my story as of right now."

Sometimes with self-doubt, all you need is someone who believes in you to say, "Keep going, you got this." I am so fortunate enough to have a close circle of friends and mentors who, when I just don't think I can, lift me up and keep me moving. Or, like the true-blue pals they are, yell, "SISUUUUUU," at me. (See upcoming chapter on Sisu.) If you have no one around you supporting your art, all is not lost. Maybe start by supporting someone else's art. Sometimes to get a friend you have to be a friend. One of my students who was very much alone in his music, started being the biggest cheerleader of the other music producers in my studio. The result? He now has at least four or five musical friends and the beginnings of a community. If opportunities aren't there, create them! Mindset.

MINDFUL MEDITATION:

> "I thrive at all times. I am valuable in all phases of my life. I am renewed in my love for life as I choose my path. I move forward with grace and ease in my artistic expression. I have all that I require to release my creativity. I am responsible for and welcome change. I am enough."

CHAPTER SUMMARY:

- Your mind will make up all kinds of reasons why 'you can't' and 'you shouldn't.'

QUESTIONS TO PONDER:

We've done a lot of pondering. Take a break and go do something that fills you up!

NOTES:

_____

_____

_____

_____

_____

_____

_____

CHAPTER 25

SISU

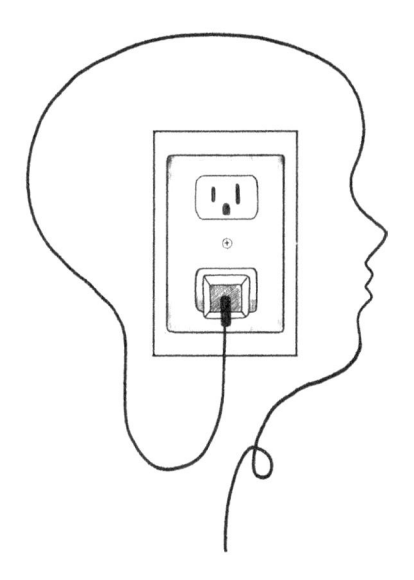

"I don't wish. I know."

Tommy Inthirath

Have you ever heard of the word sisu? Sisu is one of the most important words to a Finlander and a tremendously powerful word to adopt by an artist. I love this word, and I want to share it with you. If there are any other Finns reading this, you are probably cackling with delight right now.

Sisu means so many things. There are many popular definitions, but my favourite was penned by Elisabet Lahti, a sisu researcher, who defines sisu as, "[e]xtraordinary determination, courage, and resoluteness in the face of extreme adversity. An **action mindset** which enables individuals to **see beyond their present limitations and into what might be**. Taking action against the odds and reaching beyond observed capacities. An integral element of Finnish culture, and also a universal capacity for which the **potential exists within all individuals**."[18]

Sit for a second and read that again. Really try to grasp the concept. There are whole books written about sisu for those of you who want to explore it even more. Joanna Nylund wrote the book *Sisu: The Finnish Art of Courage*. I remember visiting my Finnish relatives in Thunder Bay and hearing the Finlanders I had just met in a Bakery say, "Heidi, you've got a lot of sisu." As a younger person, the compliment didn't really hit me because I was ignorant of all that sisu stood for. Let me unpack the essence of it by telling you a story about the Finnish people and the Winter War of 1939. You might be wondering why I am going down a rabbit hole when this book is about the arts, but I promise you we are not off-track, we are on the subject of determination and resoluteness in the face of adversity. The Soviet Union invaded Finland in November of 1939, three months after the Second World War began. Their army was massively larger than Finland's, the amount of artillery much greater, and they had well over **twenty-five hundred** tanks compared to Finland's **thirty-two**. Finland, though severely outmanned and out-supplied, held them at bay for three months in the bitter cold of winter, inflicting massive damage on this powerful army and causing international embarrassment for the Soviets. Thousands of Russian officers died of frostbite alone because they were not prepared for a drawn-out winter war. They did not have proper layers of clothing or winter tents, and because of their size, their armies had to move in a straight line on the roads. The Finnish army (which my grandfather and his brothers were a part of) cleverly dressed in white, moved around easily on skis, employed guerrilla tactics, and were much more prepared for the bitterly cold winter. Can you imagine being outside for three months in temperatures as low as minus forty degrees Celsius? It was only when ammunition and supplies were running out and exhaustion was high that the Finns pushed a peace treaty and ceded part of their land to the USSR but retained their autonomy and independence. Even though a piece of Finland was ceded (my grandfather's farm was on that land), the Finns had done the unthinkable and held their own against a far superior force, maybe even knowing that they wouldn't be able to win, I don't know. But doing all that in the middle of winter as well?[19]

This. Is. Sisu. Sisu in its most intense form means going into a battle you know you are going to lose and fighting to the death anyway! (Insert the Klingon "Qapla'!") Even now during the pandemic situation of the last two years, the concept of sisu has given me strength. It's refusing to let your spirit be dominated. Indomitable. The strength to not give up. To persevere at all costs, even if you lose. This is part of what you need as an artist to survive. You might audition for four films, get three rejections, and have to shake those off and go right into your fourth audition with full confidence engaged. You might send your new single to twenty radio stations to be rejected by them all. **Sometimes your breakthrough is in your next try**. Maybe on your twenty-first email, a theatre company will love your play and put it on. Sisu is "**perseverance**. an inner reserve of diligence, capacity, the ability to face head-on and always overcome. **Craziness**: the recklessness that inspires a person to take on something in the face of incredible odds. **Bravery, empowerment, inner strength. Gritting your teeth, continuing to fight** against an overwhelming enemy, clearing a forest with your bare hands"[20], and continuing on to win a race even after falling, like Sifan Hassan did in the women's fifteen hundred metre race in the 2021 Olympics. Did you see it? Take a moment to go on YouTube to look this up. She tripped over a fallen runner, fell down, was in last place, picked herself up, and fiercely sprinted like wildfire to win the race. I began cheering for this runner in subsequent races because I am always impressed when I see sisu in someone. Sisu means that you finish your race no matter how many times you fall along the way. Sisu.

MINDFUL MOMENT:

> "I am supported at all times. I rise to the occasion from within. I am guided in all adversity. All that comes my way is met with focus and inner strength. I am centred. I have all the help I require to move forward and thrive."

CHAPTER SUMMARY:

- Sisu. It's a powerful word that means don't give up and get back up again.
- Sometimes your breakthrough is in your next try.

QUESTIONS TO PONDER:

1) Do I finish what I start?
2) Do I run away easily when things don't go my way?

NOTES:

_____
_____
_____
_____
_____
_____
_____

CHAPTER 26

THE GREAT SACRIFICES

Sacrificing the Good for the Great

As I mentioned earlier, in my twenties, I worked as a barista in the busiest coffee shop in Winnipeg while also playing hockey on a women's recreational team, playing piano in a band, and beginning to teach music. Working as a barista hurt my body. Every minute I would have to bend down to a low fridge, pull out a big jug of milk, pour it, put the cap back on, and put it into the fridge right away again. First, it was inner forearm pain creeping up, then both thumbs started going numb, which freaked me out as I didn't know very much about the body or how nerves worked.

I started wearing wrist braces and continued to work through the pain. I discovered years later that armpit stretches are a major help to that kind of pain. If you are a dancer, you are waaaaaay better at stretching than the rest of us. As a stereotyped general rule, musicians tend to want to stretch only when something goes wrong.

In that same timeframe, hockey was also becoming more painful, with a lot of wrist action, both stick handling and shooting the puck. There came a point where I had to choose—hockey or music? Barista or music? I love coffee, and I love hockey, but it was pretty evident that neither of them were my life's arrival point (especially if you saw my wrist shot on net). I made the decision to start teaching full-time and give up my hockey team. There are moments when I miss saying hello to the same six hundred people every day, and I miss the locker room chat after the games, but sometimes **the good is the enemy of the great**. I don't know who coined that phrase, but I'll say it again—sometimes the good is the enemy of the great. If you want to be great at something, you might have to sacrifice your good. Two more goods that I have gotten rid of in my life are my harp and my cello. I love playing cello, and I have played it on stage with bands, but I am just average at it. In order for me to become great at it, it would take about ten thousand hours. If I gave up ten thousand of my hours to be great at the cello, then the things I am really supposed to be doing would suffer and be squelched. Cello is the enemy of my great. It sounds weird to say it like that, but if we spread ourselves too thin in too many different directions, we don't end up going anywhere.

Sacrifice of Money

It is so interesting to watch my students from various cultures and their different relationships with money. Some of them are racing to spend big dollars on equipment while I am holding the reins tightly and telling them they are not ready yet, and others are completely offended when I ask them to spend five dollars on sheet music for a song.

Sometimes money is the thing that will prevent you from moving forward. If you are a creative one hundred percent of the time, you will probably need to become very good at budgeting for yourself as a life in the arts isn't always the easiest thing, and your art will also require you to financially invest in it to progress. As I said before, when I hit a bad plateau, I will often pay for time with people who are ahead of me so I can keep improving. A lot of things can be learned simply through using YouTube as well. If you can get the learning for free, go for it. But sometimes in order to keep growing, money will need to be spent. Sometimes the right paint does make the difference in your product, or good shoes for dancing or clothes for an audition. Sometimes cameras, pianos, lessons, editors, and directors are needed to get your art moving. Notice I only said 'sometimes.'

I have quite a few twenty-year-old students who manage their own money and pay for weekly lessons with me. Ashley is one of them and is also one who has really learned the value of putting money responsibly into her craft so that she can expand beyond her limitations.

Ashley's Story:

"When I started in music, it was a lot easier for me to spend a hundred dollars on a night out with my friends than it was to own a nice pair of noise cancelling headphones. Spending a thousand dollars on a laptop seemed reasonable, but it was too much money when it came to buying a piano. I worked on recording on the free Garage Band for eight months because I didn't want to pay the professional Logic X price tag. The day I finally bit the bullet and purchased Logic, my musical abilities and creative potential skyrocketed. The program was more than worth it. As well, paying for my own lessons made me more motivated to do the work and to show up for myself and my music and Heidi because it was just a waste of my time and money if I didn't. In the beginning, when I wasn't putting in the right amount of effort, Heidi put my lessons on probation. She told me that she wouldn't teach me if I didn't practice because there were other people wanting my spot who were willing to work harder than I was. Yikes! I started practicing pretty quickly after I realized she was serious. I also discovered that investing in myself was the best use of my money because it meant that my product, my work, and my music would be better. It led me down the path of going to a private top-tier production school because of the experience, expertise, and information they promised. Being an artist is an expensive hobby, and an even more expensive career. It's better to pay for priceless experience and wisdom than to hoard your cash and stay stagnant."

Unfortunately, in my teaching career, I have had a couple of amazingly talented students who have been unwilling to sacrifice something for their art, and in both cases I am thinking about now, the reason was money. The first singer was a server in a loud bar, which meant that they had to speak quite loudly all evening. Their free time was also spent in loud environments. Their singing voice was/is so stunning, and I believe they could have easily had a successful career as a singer. It started with a bit of hoarseness, and then their singing range started shrinking, and then finally their entire speaking voice became hoarse. At first, they loved the rasp and said it made their sound 'extra,' but I was cautioning that it was a bad thing and told them they might need to quit their job. Giving up a job for the sake of singing seemed like 'too much.' Fast forward as things got worse, they finally went to an ear, nose, and throat (ENT) doctor to get their vocal cords examined, and sure enough, they had developed vocal nodules. For a singer, nodes are a really big deal. Nodes can require expensive surgery, and if you can afford the elective surgery, you often have to sing more cautiously afterwards so as not to reinjure. I love this singer, and they now take pristine care of their voice, steaming it and warming it up correctly, but they aren't heading toward a singing career anymore.

The other student I am thinking of came in very briefly to my studio to learn proper vocal techniques because they had chronic laryngitis that would occur every week. They had already had a voice examination, but the ENT said that there were no nodes and had no explanation for why they were losing their voice every week. I poked around and asked this extremely gifted singer what else they did in their life besides sing. They said that they were a swimming instructor two or three times a week. Boom. There it was. Yelling over splashing and kids shrieking in a pool environment without a microphone is a recipe for swollen vocal cords. I told them they didn't need better vocal exercises—what they needed to do was quit their job or teach using a microphone so they didn't have to shout for so long. This singer was also invited directly to be on a national singing television show in Canada, if that gives you a sense of their level of talent. Again, they didn't want to give up teaching swimming because it was how they made money, and it was a sense of security. They couldn't see past it, so we parted ways really quickly. There was nothing I could offer them if they truly wanted a career but weren't willing to protect their gift. The good (teaching swimming) was the enemy of the great (singing). I tell you these things because sometimes once damage has been done, especially if it's in our bodies, it is not an easy fix. This brings me to the next sacrifice . . .

Sacrificing for Your Body
Giving It What It Needs to Succeed

So we have been talking this whole time about mental health and mental obstacles, but in this chapter I also want to talk about physical health. Why? Because our physical health has a direct impact on our mental health. For so many of us artsy people, our job depends on our creativity. I am just going to go out and say it. **It is impossible to be creative when you are completely exhausted.** You can execute something like a complex combination in dance, but your creativity and enjoyment just won't be there. I can sing a song exhausted, but my emotions won't be as engaged in the lyrics, and likely, I will be just using muscle memory to make it through the song. My voice probably will be lacklustre and my singing will most likely be less enjoyable to my audience. I think that when our bodies are telling us to stop, we need to listen and allow them to recharge. It is an essential thing. For those of us who make our livings creating, treating our bodies with respect and care is one hundred percent essential to fostering the magical spark of a good idea.

On days where I have eaten an entire pizza in one sitting because of a lack of self-control, I am sluggish the rest of the day and possibly even into the next day. My body got hit with an overload of food, which takes energy to digest and break down. I am not saying eating an entire pizza in one go is a bad thing, only that there are probably consequences to it. When I stay up super late watching a suspenseful television show and am then too awake to fall asleep, I am completely bagged the next day. Last night I did a thirty-minute bike ride right before bed and was too lazy to stretch out afterwards. The result of this? Bad sleep and a sore neck this morning. If I don't exercise for a week, my body often doesn't feel energized or full of life. If I am feeling exhausted and am downing caffeine all day (my solution to feeling bagged), usually around the fourth cup my stomach starts to feel awful, and I still don't have the energy or vitality that I need for the day. Our bodies are machines, and they run on fuel. The kind of fuel you feed your body affects the way it runs. If you eat like crap, you will often feel like crap, especially the older you get. It's tempting for artists to push through on caffeine, but then you are running on borrowed energy and taxing your adrenal glands. The result is adrenal exhaustion. I recommend reading the book *This is Your Brain on Food* by Uma Naidoo, which talks about the amazing gut/brain connection and how food and digestion affect energy and mood.

If I am feeling extreme fatigue from my food choices, it is really hard to disassociate that feeling from depression. Fatigue and depression feel almost the same to me. If I've made some poor food or sleep choices, the next day I need to prepare myself for the consequence of that decision, which for me is usually lethargy and moodiness. The next day I take care to remind myself that I am not having a mental health breakdown, everything is okay, it's just going to be a more tired day. On tired days I like to do a lot of things that are on my non-creative to-do list. Examples would be dying my hair, cleaning, gardening, grocery shopping, or cooking. These are all things that don't need creative artistic energy (at least not the way I cook). On days like that, I like to get all the time-consuming tasks out of the way so that once I have had a good sleep and feel refreshed physically, I can get back to creating artistic things with a lighter load.

Some days, however, your body is so exhausted that it's important to listen to it and maybe take a couch day. My body is super sensitive to certain foods, and sometimes what I eat causes my stomach to inflame and my energy levels to crash. Sometimes on a day off when I have a list of things I want to accomplish, unfortunately, my energy levels are low, which again, feels the same as depression to me. I will go through my process for you. I used to panic and have thoughts like, 'Am I depressed? How are my emotions today?' Then after a minute, I rationalized to myself, 'Heidi, you are not depressed, you are just fatigued.' Now, I purposely take a moment to say to myself, 'This is okay. Rest is okay. I am okay.' To avoid feelings of guilt or shame, I lower my expectations for the day. In those moments, I have a choice to be angry at myself or my body for not doing what I want it to in the day, but honestly, that kind of thinking does really little. The anger and frustration I allow to surface does not change my current state of energy, and it does not change what I chose to eat yesterday or how my body reacted. What it does change is my mental health for the day, and sometimes my week. This kind of guilt and anger at myself is not beneficial to my mind, emotions, or body. If you study this kind of thing, you can research the long-term effects of fear, anger, and guilt on your physical body. My good friend and mentor JoAnn has told me that my body is a part of me, and that I need to remember that it is doing the best it can for me at that moment. Thinking that way allows me to have compassion and gratitude for my body, which is doing its best with what it's been given and how I've treated it. I am learning to be peaceful with my rest days, to not feel guilty for streaming multiple seasons of a show on the couch and napping the day away. This seems to be in contradiction with my chapter on escaping reality and dealing with distractions, but I assure you, it is not. Using media as an escape from accomplishing the things of your heart is one thing, but when your body is exhausted and you are burnt out, there needs to be recovery time. If you are blessed with super high energy levels like my brother Stephen and his wife then your ability to run is greater than mine. But even then, you still need to pay attention to what your body is telling you and when it is saying "rest." Rest is a gift to your body. You get to live in your body for another sixty plus years for some of you. You might as well make that journey a fulfilling one!

> *"If you don't take time for your wellness, you will be forced to take time for your illness."*
>
> ## *Joyce Sunada*[21]

For my student Denika, who deals with some fairly substantial health issues, planning and leaving a large amount of margin was essential in order for her to do her monthly sings with our Pass the Performance. She was a master at this and didn't miss a month. Sometimes intentionality plays a part when health is unpredictable. Here she is to tell you herself . . .

Denika's Story:

"Music in my life has become a bit different this year. I essentially have an undiagnosed sickness that comes in the form of really painful sores in my mouth and throat. They aren't always there, but they seem to pop up at random times without any sort of clear pattern. I always need to be prepared to take a minimum of two weeks off to recover without being able to eat, sing, or talk. It's been a journey of tests, tests, and more tests and still not having any definite answers. I am part of Heidi's PTP Instagram sings, but because I never know when I will be well enough to sing, it means making sure I have my monthly video recorded well in advance, and even a couple of 'just in case' videos finished. I send my videos to Heidi really early just so that I know I won't miss out on the chance to perform. Honestly, you never really miss something until it's gone. Sure, I've always known music is a big part of my life, but when all of a sudden I don't even have the option to sing, it's almost like there's a gaping hole in my life. I've grown as a person tremendously through all of this. Music is a constant source of life for me during those weeks when I'm sick, and on special days when enough energy is available, trips to the piano are made. It's hard not being able to speak words, sing lyrics, or send that verbal message out into the world, but I find that sometimes just playing out my feelings on the piano can speak volumes to my day. I think my number one piece of advice would be, if you are truly passionate about your art, then you can find a way even in the face of an obstacle like sickness. You don't have to be sitting at a piano and belting out words for you to be 'making good music.'

"One of Heidi's rules that I carry nearest and dearest to my heart is the 'I can't' rule. Basically . . . don't ever say, 'I can't.' If you are really serious about wanting to join that choir or about learning how to paint, then don't give up. Keep trying. Keep learning. Now, you may not necessarily be able to play like everyone else. Some things, like my sickness, are simply out of our control, but I want to encourage you to find another way. I know it's cliché, but if you can be your own kind of beautiful, I'm pretty sure you can manage to play your own kind of music."

I will never forget my first lesson with the next student, Tyson. He did not tell me he was dyslexic until the second or third piano lesson when he was still having trouble differentiating between the keys.

Tyson's Story:

"Growing up, in school, I always had to be in a separate class because I couldn't do what the other kids were doing. For spelling, I was always two grades lower than everyone else was. This made me feel really unworthy and not valuable and not needed. I always required help for the work I was doing and didn't really do anything on my own. I didn't even know why I needed help. I finally found out I had dyslexia in grade eight, which was good, but hard because it affirmed that I was different and that there was 'something wrong with me.' It was actually really hard because I wanted to be the same as other people, and I wasn't. I've definitely accepted it a lot more and if people talk to me about it now, it's not as discouraging as it used to be. When I started taking music lessons, I didn't know how much dyslexia would affect me with the piano. I think it's gone pretty well so far and hasn't been that much of a disadvantage, and I just finished writing my first song. I would say if you think you might have a disability, go and see if you do first of all. If you do, just keep trying new things, and try not to get discouraged. There are plenty of other people that struggle with the same thing you do. And there's always help."

Sacrifice for Mental Health

Sometimes life happens hard. When things get that way, everything around you can feel like it is spinning and spiralling out of your control. I was recently in this place when my mother fell ill and was taken to the hospital while I was finishing my teaching year. My original goal was to have this book finished by the beginning of July 2021, but my plans needed to change to fit the needs of my family. My mother being sick required me to pack up my recording equipment in a day and drive eighteen hours straight in a car with a cat so I could care for her and be present for my father. Life happens. In these situations, your mental health takes priority over your art. Sometimes because of a problem in brain chemistry or genetic makeup, everything starts caving in on you. I have taught a couple of students who have been in this place. Sometimes I didn't see it because most of these brave souls are very good at hiding their depression or their crippling anxiety. I am grateful to teach these ones as well as it teaches me to live outside of what I think I know and become more aware and empathetic. Mental illnesses are no joke and need to be addressed. If you are struggling with crippling panic attacks, eating disorders, self-harming, and/or intense depression, it is a good idea to deal with or learn to cope with that first and use your art as a way to come alongside and support your healing. I believe the pursuit of happiness and self-love takes precedence. There is nothing wrong with shifting your focus away from your art for a time to get help for these things. It does not mean you won't return to pursuing your craft professionally, that you can't enjoy it through the process of healing, that you aren't called to create, or that you can't be who you want to be. You can. You can. You can. But don't run away from those bigger things. Talk about them with family, close friends, a doctor, a therapist, etc. I talk about therapy with students that might need it and describe it as a toothbrush for your heart. In the same way that you keep your mouth clean with a toothbrush so you don't get tooth decay, therapy can keep you from getting heart decay. Iris is a phenomenal athlete who loves drawing, music, cats, and all things creative. There was a moment, however, during the pandemic when things got really tough and it took me a second to notice.

Iris's Story:

"There comes a time when life gets out of hand, and you may need to put your art on pause. When my life was spinning out of control, music, something that I love, turned into a negative and something that felt like a heavy weight on my chest. Art should be the opposite of that. Art should feed your soul. In the moment my life was out of control, I would continuously put off this musical project I was working on, which had a deadline. This procrastination made the weight on my chest even heavier as every day I kept avoiding what I needed to get done. I realized that because of the stress and anxiety in my life, I needed to take a step back from music and performing to work on me. Once you fix or find ways to deal with your stress and anxiety, then you can bring your art back into your life. Some people may use creativity as a way to help them with their stress and anxiety, but if you're like me, then you may feel as though practicing and having goals makes that stress and anxiety worse. In times like these, we must stop, take a break, and make sure our mental health is good before we take on projects that may add to it in a negative way. To everyone that has felt this or is going through this right now, I know saying that sounds like the typical mental health speech, but it really is true. There are lots of resources to reach out to where there are people who are more than happy to help you out. This could even include your family members, friends, or hotlines that you can call to help you calm down. Lastly, as simple as it is, breathe."

Victoria Patterson – Dancer, Dance Instructor, Administrator

"Home life and school life come into the studio and highly affect dancers in a dance class. Some of our students are here for six to ten hours a week, so we see a lot of them. If their home life is suffering, they will often resort to missing classes, which brings the mood of the whole class down. In my studio, we work really hard to build relationships with our dancers so that they can express themselves when things are tough. They will often come up to us and say, 'I failed my test, and I feel miserable,' and I think that's a win for us because we can empathize with them, and then help them to have a good dance class. If they're open about their struggles with us, letting it out helps them move past it. Keeping their pain bottled inside is very toxic in a dance class. Just having that open relationship and conversation changes the mood completely for how they're going to act that evening."

I describe negative emotions to my students as being like potatoes. Yes. I actually heard someone say this in Toronto in my twenties, and I have never forgotten it. Do you know what happens to potatoes if you leave them long enough in your cupboard? At first, they may sprout, but if you leave them long enough, they liquify and go rancid. Yum. Why are we talking about liquified, rancid potatoes? Because like emotions, if you keep them stored up in the cupboard of your heart without learning to process them or express them, they will liquify and go rancid and will affect you as a human being and also as an artist. Instead, it is important that you do something active with them. Cut them up, make french fries, mash them, but acknowledge them and get them out somehow. I have used therapy three times in my twenties to process and work through pain that was causing my life's heartbeat to be at a standstill. I don't see any of that time as having been wasted time either. It was necessary work needed to clean out some of the potato sludge of pain and bitterness that was residing in me. For you younger readers who are still on your guardians' health plans, therapy can cost as little as five dollars per hour. The way I look at it, the younger you can get help for emotions that you are not able to process, the sooner you can build new patterns of coping and strategy for the rest of your life and artistic career. It is often much harder at age seventy to learn new mental health skills, so do so while you are young so that you can live out as much freedom as possible. Regardless of where my art takes me, I want to live my life to the fullest, enjoying everything that life has for me and not holding back.

MINDFUL MEDITATION:

"I love myself. I respect all that my body, mind, spirit, and soul require to thrive. My heart speaks, and I listen. I trust my inner voice to regulate my own personal health and welfare. I gift myself with time well-spent working through emotional blocks. I am renewed physically, emotionally, and spiritually. I focus on what is important."

CHAPTER SUMMARY:

- If you love and treasure something, sometimes you have to sacrifice for it.

QUESTIONS TO PONDER:

1) Am I giving my creativity what it needs to flourish?

2) Are there habits I have that are harming my gift? If so, what keeps me from letting go of them?

NOTES:

CHAPTER 27
SOCIAL MEDIA AVOIDANCE

"I have nothing to share. Who do I share this with? Social media is a whole other world that I don't want to be a part of. I am already part of a world that's real, that's living.
It is a waste of time. I am not familiar with it and don't like sharing a lot of my own things with people that I don't know. It might be wrong."

Anonymous Student

Social media can be many things. It can be toxic, my marketing strategy, a newspaper, and also my connection with people I love. It can also be an angry rage session with everyone on Facebook chiming in with nasty opinions. But I would say that if you are a creative, social media is also a necessary tool. The key is to have it working **for you** and not **owning you**. This is a big issue for me and was something at the beginning of 2022 that I decided to gain some control over. A tendency of mine is to start scrolling through other people's things on a work break, and then lose an hour a day. Sometimes I have felt like my phone owned me, especially in the five hundred days of Pass the Performance when I had to text students constantly for their videos. If I am being honest with you, I still haven't found my balance here or the 'right amount.' As I write this, I am off platforms but am still checking my messages. In the last two weeks, I have been so much more productive, and I am so happy with myself. Am I missing out? I am not sure yet. I definitely feel like I am in a Heidi-cave and don't know what's been going on in anyone's lives. I wish I had the answer for you, but I am human, and this is one that I am still learning how to manage and balance. That being said, I have many friends who use it successfully for their business and their art, so rather than leaving you without any brilliant thought at all, I am inviting my friend Rebecca King to 'the stage' to talk to you about social media.

Rebecca King – International Speaker, Founder of Invictus Prophetic

"My relationship with social media revolves around two things. One of them is my friends that I have around the world, real friends. The other is work related. In both of those worlds, I have a significant social media presence and use it for advertising, networking, and now broadcasting. At this point, social media is a major player around the world as far as influence goes, and I couldn't keep working without it.

"There have been times when social media has driven me absolutely crazy because of extremism, especially in North America in the last four or five years. I realized at a certain point that **I was in control of my online presence,** and I began to delete people who would disrespect my views, make nasty remarks, or who would become politically charged. I learned that I could be in control. And I think that's what a lot of young people need to realize: social media is a tool that is for good, as long as you're in control of it.

"Sometimes it's a bit more difficult for a person of a younger age to understand that they have to regulate social media for themselves because the world is as it is right now. For example, if someone posts something hate-filled or that stirs things up so that people become reactive instead of responsive, I delete them. That's me taking power of my own online environment instead of running away—recognizing that social media is part of the world, this is how we live, and that we need to regulate it for ourselves as best as possible.

"For young creatives afraid of social media, I think the issues aren't with social media at all. I think that it is much deeper and bigger. It's often a problem of identity, and it just presents as being social media-related. All of us have those things to work out. Some of the social pressure that they experience puts them in a place where they are afraid. **I look back to my youth and most of my fears were peer-related, and social media is definitely a peer-related thing.**"

Upon thinking about it, I absolutely agree with Rebecca that fear of social media is an internal thing that only manifests as fear. There are negative beliefs in there and the result is the behaviour. Another one of my student's feelings toward social media is in line with that. They told me they were afraid of posting anything because they were afraid that people would judge what they were doing and think they were weird, that they wouldn't be seen as interesting, that they wouldn't get the number of likes that they wanted, or that people would judge the amount of likes and follows they got, and then judge them as a person as a result.

Most of those things have to do with identity. There are so many sides to social media. For me, it is a distraction, which doesn't mean social media is bad, it actually means my self-discipline is lacking and that I give social media too many hours of my day. Obviously, we as creatives are going to need to become masters at this because **social media does equal influence.**

There is also another type of person who says to me, "I would rather be in reality and with real people and not post my life online." I think it is fine to be disinterested in having an online presence if you have a really rich and full life and don't want to make time for it, as long as you are not a creative or an influencer with your art as your business. When it comes to self-promotion, or promotion of events and activities, how else are you going to do it? If you are in a dance ensemble, it might be easier to get away with staying offline and letting your company do the promotion work. But if it's your product, your art show, or your new single, you are going to have to become comfortable using social media for your business. Start small and watch tutorials and YouTube videos on how to use the different platforms effectively to promote your work. It's a journey, you don't have to be perfect at it.

> "Art isn't complete until you've shared it with someone. That doesn't mean you have to show everything to everyone. Creativity is an intimate process. But there is a point where you need to take the risk, to be vulnerable to someone. Art connects us on a different level.
> It holds and releases mystical power. Art makes us brave."
>
> **Shannon Schultz**

MINDFUL MEDITATION:

"I am safe to express my art publicly. I choose to risk. I am safe to step out and am propelled forward. I embrace my journey in my artistic expression. I control my time with wisdom. I am divinely directed. I am stable and centred."

CHAPTER SUMMARY:

- You are in control of your online environment.
- You are the regulator.
- Social media is sometimes a necessary tool for the creative.
- Art is meant to be shared.
- Mental health always takes priority.

QUESTIONS TO PONDER:

1) What is my relationship with social media? Am I using it as an escape, an addiction, or a tool? Am I using it at all? Why? Why not?

2) Does social media feel safe to me? Why or why not?

NOTES:

_____
_____
_____
_____
_____
_____
_____
_____

CHAPTER 28
ADVICE FROM PROFESSIONALS IN THE FIELD

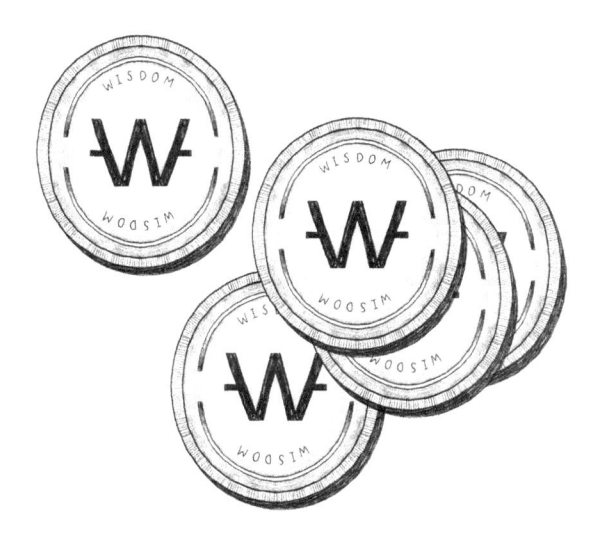

The following words from these professionals are life changing. Take your time reading each one, gleaning the golden nuggets from these amazing creatives and what they are giving away to you.

Charles Patton II - Red Lion Spoken Word Artist, Poet

"Art can purely be 'I just want to express how I feel,' in which case, there isn't as much pressure to create. But when you start operating at a higher level where you are getting bookings and jobs, it adds a bit more stress. You feel as an artist that you have to meet the expectations of the people hiring you because now you have an audience, fans, and people that listen to you, and they expect something out of you, so it adds pressure to force things out of you. You're not focused on the subject matter anymore; you're focused on the people. Which for me cuts off creativity. Whenever I don't force things to come out, and I just sit there and meditate, nine times out of ten, it just comes out after a while. Art and nature are not supposed to be stressful. But whenever it turns into income, it adds that stress. For me personally, I've had to learn to say no to things that I am not prepared for, even though they have been offered to me. Even if the pay is great, you compromise your credibility if it's a bad fit and doesn't end up coming across as any good. It's good to recommend other people you know who fit that mould. Art is bigger than just me. I know we have this mentality of, 'Hey, I've got to get mine,' and it's not bad to want things for yourself. But in the larger grand scheme of things, whenever your identity is tied to your art, you lose your compassion and sense of community with other people because you are so focused on building your own thing, when in actuality, it is those very relationships with other people that can help expand you and build you."

Victoria Patterson – Dancer, Dance Instructor, Administrator

"You have to follow your heart. Don't let anything stop you along the way if this is actually something you want to do and pursue. If you want to work toward something, keep going regardless if you don't have the money to do so, the facility, or the support around you. Don't let those things stop you. Find the right people to look up to and surround yourself with ones who are on the same page as you, that motivate you to be better, and who are heading toward the same goal as you. Being the only artist in a group of friends or family, that's hard. You need to find people who you can relate to and who can help you. You need that community. You need that support. If you don't have that support, don't quit, just go and find it for yourself."

Stacey James – Canadian Singer-Songwriter, Recording Artist

"I would say that the one thing that is most important, that really stands out to me, is that no matter what, just keep expressing yourself through art. And the reason I say that is because I had a number of people tell me, 'Yeah, you should probably never get on stage with a keyboard,' or 'You know what? I just don't think that people are going to connect with your writing,' or 'You should probably just make things very different.' I listened, and I thought, *I'll hear you, and I'll take the constructive criticism parts, but I am going to allow this to be my fuel and craft my artistry the way that I feel is most necessary because I am so passionate about it. I'm not going to stop.* If I had listened, I would never have been on stage for the last eight years with my keyboard. I never would have been to different cities and played with my band if I had listened to everyone around me. So make sure you listen to your heart and your soul when it comes to you as an artist or writer. And stay plugged into yourself as a being because that is probably the most important thing, and I truly wish somebody would have told me that because it probably would have saved me a little bit of heartache in the past. That would be my advice to you."

Emily Solstice Tait – Dancer

"Remember that there are many different ways to focus on your dance form. Pay attention to what excites you and follow it on social media, go through company websites, follow artists that you are inspired by, and then do something about that. Find your dance (or art form) community, even if it looks different than what you trained in. Build plans and schedules for your goals, and don't be afraid to contact artists or companies looking for a chance to watch a rehearsal, train, or audition. Help them find passionate artists for their projects by doing the work of introducing yourself to them. Lastly, when it comes time, ask for mentorship on organizing your finances as an artist. Work as a community!"

Patric Scott – Swiss Singer-Songwriter, Independent Recording Artist

"Think a little bit more about the business side, if you are serious, and if you are willing to spend some money on the production of a single or an EP, or even an album. It's a lot of money that you invest there, and you also really need a business plan for that side of it, which means using social media. If you don't have money for a music video, you can do something else. You can sit and film yourself with the guitar or piano singing the song. Or maybe get together and involve some friends—be creative. Inspire yourself. With social media, have a plan. For example, if your project is coming out in June, start with the first post at the end of May. Ask friends to cover the song. There are so many things you can do. And this is really important. What I tell all my students and all my artists—go to the open mics. Check out songwriting circles. There you can go and perform live. Then you have the social media part and the old-school part of going on stage. It's also important to have a business card so that people know who you are on stage. The card should have your name, website, Instagram, and any other social media information on it. Then you have a good chance of building up your career.

"Success. So many people ask me what success means to me. It is to pay my bills with my singing. When I was able to do this, it was a huge success for me! Of course, it is also working with different people. I love co-writing. I worked with Naturally Seven, an acapella band, which was a dream come true.

"You have to work your butt off, it's true. In the end, when you work and you do your best, I promise you will get more and more attention from people, either because of your social media work or your work onstage. Even for me, I rehearse every day. I do my exercises every morning and I know to keep at it, because I have been through all my chapters of being signed by a record company, and also having my own label. If you have a passion for what you are doing, you will do it."

Cypha Diaz – Hip-hop Artist, DJ, Founder of Cyph Life and Dim Mak

"Whatever your field is, be comfortable there. Live there. Expand there. Don't be scared to grow there. This is what you do. This is who you are. This is your essence. Embrace it. Embrace who you are. Love who you are. Embrace your individuality. Your individualism is everything. There is no other you. You're the only you that has ever been made, which is crazy. So exploit that, and love yourself and all your weirdness.

"Use your resources. Use what you have available. Use each other. Create bands. Create groups. Promote each other. Use your people. Make it so your people can use you. This social media thing is real, and you can use it as a tool to get yourself ahead if you use it right. So I would advise that you use each other.

"Also, stay laser light focused. Practice your craft, hone your craft, and become a master at your craft. Master your tool. If you're a singer, then get yourself to the peak performance level that you can find. Practice, practice, practice. How do you get to Carnegie Hall? Practice! Stay consistent. Consistency is key. You stay on the ball like that. Stay positive. Keep your heart rate up. Do something every day to get your heart rate pumping, whether it's going for a run or a walk, doing some jumping jacks, or going for a swim or a bike ride even. Anything to get your mind, your body, and your soul fit. Keep your mind limber, and keep your brain open to new possibilities. Don't forget to enjoy life. You only have one. Smile. Play your hearts out. Do what you do to get by. There ain't no tellin' how far you can get. Salut. Love."

Doug Wamble – Guitarist, Producer, Jazz Musician, Songwriter

"If I could give one piece of advice, it would be in two parts. My initial love was to be a jazz guitar player. That's all I wanted to do. I wanted to be in New York, and I wanted to play jazz music. But I learned that that wasn't always going to be the sum total of my musical life. So I decided to branch out a little bit, and I learned how to use recording software and virtual instruments. I learned how to produce, how to write, and how to sing. All these things that were going to be helpful to me in diversifying my career. But that never really took away from my first love and my passion for being a better jazz musician. I love the history of jazz music so much, and I still practice it today. I still love listening to Thelonius Monk and Charlie Parker and learning from them. So my advice would be to have a very clear goal and purpose as to what you want to be as a musician, but also realize that you have to have a big skill set. Even before the pandemic, I was doing lots of things—film composition, writing for television commercials, being someone else's guitar player, and singing. All these kinds of things really helped me sustain a life and feed my family for many years. But it didn't take away from the fact that I was really pursuing an artistic goal of being a really good musician, the best I could be. So find your path, and be very clear about what that path is. But understand that the path may not lead you to the destination that you want it to, or that you thought it would. But just be open to it and be as good as you can at whatever you do. And be grateful. Every time you get to play music is a gift. There are people out there with no hands, no voice boxes, no ability to hear, and no homes. So every time you get to create is a privilege. If you approach that with gratitude and love for music, then by default you will be a success because you will be making joyful music."

Samantha Katz – Photographer, Photography Business Educator

"When I started out, I loved too many different types of photography to keep myself from shooting it all, so I went against the norm, and I didn't niche down.

"If you are starting out your photography career, you might be thinking this is the exact opposite of what you have been told. Well, I was told the same thing when I started out, and now, ten years into my career, I can tell you confidently that you shouldn't pick a niche. Not picking a niche allowed me to explore, try different types of photography, force myself to do new things all the time, be uncomfortable, and be forced to learn a variety of skills. Not niching down made me try so many things that I found out exactly what I love and what I didn't love to shoot very quickly.

Not niching down allowed me to create a vast portfolio that showcased my range, and more often than not, I had an example.

"Not niching down opened me up to take every single job that came my way, and I needed the work, not just for the money but to get better. After years of not niching down, my niche happened on its own. The work that I loved the most and that I felt the proudest of naturally became what I shared, and therefore more and more people continued to book me for this kind of work. If you are starting your career in photography, my advice to you is not to niche down . . . yet!

"Fall in love with photography. Say YES to every single opportunity to get behind the camera. Seek shoots that you have ZERO experience in, and put yourself in front of every single shooting chance you get. Your niche will pick you."

Arielle Jodine – Singer-Songwriter, Studio Alumni

"What is your definition of success? As a creative, this is one of the biggest questions you need to answer for yourself.

"To be a *creative* requires a mind shift. Whatever you think the definition of success is . . . change it. I mean this in the nicest way possible, but if your definition of success is in line with what the industry says, you're in for an uphill battle, my friend. According to industry standards, success looks a certain way. Getting a record deal with a fancy label, millions of streams on Spotify, and one of your songs becoming a trending sound on TikTok. What do you think success is? Is it what I've just listed, or is it simply creating in the first place? Is it taking a risk and putting your art out into the world? Is it the accomplishment of fashioning something you're proud of?

"It was never my dream to release music. I'm a singer, a songwriter, and a creative, but I never thought recording and releasing songs was something I wanted to do. With a lot of encouragement from the author of this book, we took the steps needed to get my songs from basic ideas into fully produced songs.

"I independently recorded, financed, and released a five-song EP (*Wherever He Goes* by Arielle Jodine on all streaming platforms, shameless plug). According to industry standards, it was an utter failure. And I mean failure! I worked hard to get it played on the radio, printed CDs to sell, did an album release party, made my pitch to Spotify, but in the end . . . I made pennies in streams, I never made it onto a Spotify playlist, and though I did make it on the radio (which is still super exciting to this day!), plays rarely turn into revenue.

"That initial rush of friends and family listening to your art dwindles after a couple of weeks, and you're faced with the question, was this even worth all my time and money? I initially thought the definition of success would be to break even. If I could make the money back that I put into the project, then I would be able to continue forward making music. But that can't be my definition either, because that sure didn't happen!

"To be a *creative* is not always an easy road. It takes time, constant reflection, taking risks (like outrageous amounts of risks!), and being okay with never 'going anywhere.'

"I'll be honest, I'm not at the end of this journey where I can say that I have fully changed my definition of success and can confidently put out music whether anyone streams it or not. But I am still taking risks and releasing my art to the world! I wouldn't regret it for a second, but it requires constant reflection on what I define success as. When it comes down to it, I am successful for simply doing it.

"I'll just say it, YOU are successful for being YOU. I almost sound a little motivational speaker-esque, but I'm serious! If you did it, if you're in the middle of doing it, or if it is only a spark of the first creative idea, you're doing it! You're making it! You're creating! You're successful! You don't know me, but trust me . . . that thing you made . . . it's stunning."

CHAPTER SUMMARY:

- Don't be afraid to turn down an opportunity that is a bad fit. Doing a sloppy job will only hurt your reputation as an artist.

- Create your own community for support if none exists.

- Do something every day to get your heart rate up. Keep your soul and body healthy.

- Don't be afraid to have a bunch of artistic side hustles while still following your main love. It is a blessing to be able to support yourself with your art.

- Be open to trying different styles within your realm, and allow your niche to find you.

- You are successful if you are creating, authentic, and love what you do.

QUESTIONS TO PONDER:

1) After reading this book, what is your definition of success? Has it changed?

2) Do you have a community to inspire you? If not, where can you go to find one?

3) What job opportunities are available for you in your chosen field? Are there any that maybe you haven't considered that you could do on the side as well as having your main love?

NOTES:

CHAPTER 29

CLOSING THOUGHTS AND A GOOD MOUSE STORY

So we're nearing the end of all that I want to say to you in this book. Some of you might be thinking this is going to be a lot of work, and you're right, mental health as an artist does take work. Mental health for anybody takes work. I think we are so blessed because our very profession forces us to look inward and deal with a lot of these issues in order to succeed. If you are working as an envelope stuffer (one of my high school jobs), it isn't necessary for your envelope stuffing to do internal work. I look at all the internal work I have been forced to do as a creative in order to survive, and I can see how it has made my life SO. MUCH. BETTER. Fear is not fun. Embarrassment is not fun. Extreme perfectionism is not fun. I love that being a creative has forced a higher level of mindfulness, self-acceptance, self-discipline, and achievement out of me. I absolutely believe it's going to do the same thing for you. Am I saying that I am never anxious? No. Am I saying that I am perfect? Definitely not. Am I saying that there's not a struggle? No. What I am saying is I am grateful for the fact that I am in the struggle!

To prevent the 'I'll never get there' syndrome, I would encourage you to work on only the **one** roadblock that is interfering with your creativity right now. If you have none and you are good, don't look at the ones that you 'think' could maybe apply to you—just deal with any obstacle that comes up as it does. So much of your journey will simply be to look ahead, keep your eyes on your own lane, and keep moving forward in your lane. And remember, **sometimes roadblocks in your path are springboards meant to take you higher**. You either have to **quit** or **level up** to get over them.

An analogy that I have heard for many years is that of the baby eagles learning how to fly. Sometimes the baby eagles are so content in their nests that they have no desire to learn how to fly, no desire for greater things. What the parent eagles do to encourage flight is to remove all the soft things slowly from the nest, making it less desirable and less cozy. That safe nest starts to become uncomfortable, with sharp edges and thorns poking out, and that is what leads the eagles to leave it and attempt to fly. In your life, watch for those moments where your situation that felt like home for so long begins to feel foreign and confining. Personally, I dislike the 'uncomfortable' stage SO much. But after I have learned to fly, I am often filled with gratitude for the new and higher place.

If you have made it this far, I saved the best story for last—your reward for making it to the end.

The first house I ever rented was one of the smallest houses you have ever seen in North America—well under five hundred square feet. I am not sure how many years I lived there, but in my last year there, all of a sudden, the foundation of the house shifted. This caused a fairly large mouse problem in the unfinished rock dungeon of a basement. I talked to my landlord, and he put mouse poison in the basement and filled it with traps. I kept throwing the mice in the garbage and buying new traps. I found mouse poop in so many personal items, even in my own bedroom. Mice ruined my baseball glove, my family Christmas ornaments, crochet blankets, etc., etc. Still, I was content to live there, making life work week to week, because my mind was thinking small and was contained within the tiny yellow mouse house. Thank God for what happened next. The moment my situation became unbearable was when a drunk mouse who had eaten poison from the basement came out from **underneath the piano between a student's feet** DURING A MUSIC LESSON.

Horrifying moment for me, big smile for you. The student didn't see it, but I shrieked quickly, captured the slow-moving wobbly mouse, and threw it outside. Pause. This was the thing I had feared most once the house began having mouse issues, and it had just happened. That was the moment that my situation became so uncomfortable that I levelled up, told my landlord that day that I was out of there, no matter what he did to fix the foundation, and I moved into an amazing home with quadruple the room for the next four years.

Sometimes roadblocks are springboards to take you higher, to level up.

You've made it through ten years of my teaching journey! There are whole books written on each topic that is discussed here, but *On the Edge of Greatness* was designed to be an overview of all the things I have encountered as an educator so that you can see the big picture, discover what applies to you, hear courageous stories from my students, AND realize you are not alone. Thank you so much for buying this book, and I would love to hear how it has impacted you as an artist.

Keep Going. You got this.
Heidi Korte

ENDNOTES

1. Shoshana Bean, "Shoshana Bean," "Chat about my masterclasses!!!", Facebook, May 26, 2017, https://www.facebook.com/shoshanabean/videos/1015515371548642

2. *Ibid.*

3. Pablo Picasso, "Famous Pablo Picasso Quotes," Pablo Picasso – Paintings, Quotes, & Biography, (accessed October 2022), https://www.pablopicasso.org/quotes.jsp

4. Brassaï (Gyula Halász), "Quotes by Brassai," Photo Quotes, (accessed October 2022), https://photoquotes.com/author/brassai

5. Pope John Paul II, "Top 50 Pope John Paul II Quotes," quotefancy, (accessed October 2022), https://quotefancy.com/quote/891366/Pope-John-Paul-II-The-purpose-ofart-is-nothing-less-than-the-upliftment-of-the-human

6. Johnny Cash, "Johnny Cash talks addiction and prisons, 1975: CBC Archives," Youtube, December 14, 2009, https://www.youtube.com/watch?v=NAjtk3scqZY&t=245s. See Especially timestamp 3:12.

7. "Lena Horne on Rosie O'Donnell 1997," Youtube, June 22, 2008, https://www.youtube.com/watch?v=q_8hyO29wWk&t=301s

8. Jack Frost, *From Spiritual Slavery to Spiritual Sonship*. Destiny Image, 2006.

9. Aubrey Logan, "So Cute," from the album *Where the Sunshine is Expensive*, 2020, https://aubreylogan.com/song/b0d88208ba/so-cute

10. Shoshana Bean, "Shoshana Bean," "Chat about my masterclasses!!!", Facebook, May 26, 2017, https://www.facebook.com/shoshanabean/videos/1015515371548642

11. Peck, M. Scott. *The road less traveled: A new psychology of love, traditional values, and spiritual growth*. Simon and Schuster, 2002.

12. Harmon Okinyo, "Harmon Okinyo > Quotes > Quotable Quote," Goodreads, 2022 (accessed October 2022), https://www.goodreads.com/quotes/7322221-time-is-a-currency-you-canonly-spend-once-so

13. "Carol Burnett Discusses The People She Won't Work With | The Dick Cavett Show," Youtube, July 16, 2021, https://www.youtube.com/watch?v=V49ZuOb_Hr0&t=119s

14. Paul Williams, quoted in "Story Behind the Song: 'The Rainbow Connection'," video interview by *The Tennessean*, October 3, 2016 (accessed October 2022), https://www.youtube.com/watch?v=ka2DTKjrknc

15. Jessica I. Morales, "The Heart's Electromagnetic Field Is Your Superpower," *Psychology Today*, November 29, 2020, https://www.psychologytoday.com/intl/blog/building-the-habit-hero/202011/the-hearts-electromagnetic-field-is-your-superpower (accessed October 2022)

16. *Friends*, Episode 231, "The One Where Joey Speaks French," Directed by Gary Halvorson, written by Sherry Bilsing-Graham & Ellen Plummer, first aired February 19, 2004.

17. Douglas Lumsden, https://twitter.com/DouglasLumsden1/status/1417189409527517186 (accessed October 2022)

18. Elisabet Lahti, Definition of Sisu, https://www.facebook.com/InspireSisu/photos/a.559419074076964/1193459634006235/ (accessed October 2022)

19. For information on the Winter War please see https://en.wikipedia.org/wiki/Winter_War and its references, and https://www.iwm.org.uk/history/a-short-history-of-the-winter-war.

20. Definition of Sisu, by Martha'sCellmate, Urban Dictionary, November 11, 2004, https://www.urbandictionary.com/define.php?term=Sisue. (More specific source info not given.)

21. Joyce Sunada, "Huddle," thompsonbooks, Thompson Educational Publishing, Inc., 2022 (accessed October 2022), http://thompsonbooks.com/kto12/h/huddle/ripple-effect/

THANK YOU

Thank you so much to all the professionals who helped this project by sharing wisdom with the next generation and giving interviews. You are such an important part of this book. Thank you.

JoAnn McFatter
Iris Bjornson
Dane Bjornson
Natasha Boone
Kevan Kenneth Bowkett
Therese Curatolo
Cypha Diaz
Ray Hughes
Stacey James
Samantha Katz
Rebecca King
Jon Loeppky
Camille Meub
Julie Meyer
Jack Mills
Ryan Nealon
Bret Paddock
Victoria Patterson
Charles Patton II
Haven Peckover
Wendy Peter
Glenn Radley

Maggie Regimbal
Shannon Schultz
Patric Scott
Emily Solstice Tait
Paige Uttley
Doug Wamble

Special thanks to:
Sid and Bea Dueck
Stephen and Melissa Korte
Bob Hill
Steve Brown
Linda and Peter Korte
Cathy Dueck
For helping make this book a reality and supporting the project financially.

Thank you so much to my students who helped this project by contributing and sharing their stories, as well as all you students over the last ten years who have made my musical journey richer and better. I have been changed.

Printed by BoD"in Norderstedt, Germany